JOYFUL CATS
COLORING BOOK
VOLUME II
THIRTY DRAWINGS TO COLOR

FIRST EDITION

THANK YOU VERY MUCH FOR PURCHASING THIS COLORING BOOK.

DESIGNED FOR BOTH THE BEGINNER AND INTERMEDIATE COLORING LEVELS,

THIS COLORING BOOK FEATURES SOME OF MY BEST CAT DRAWINGS.

DEDICATED TO SOPHIA, ANNE AND ELENA.

THANK YOU FOR INSPIRING ME TO BE THE BEST ARTIST I CAN BE ALWAYS!

ENJOY, AND LET YOUR ARTISTIC SIDE SHINE THROUGH!

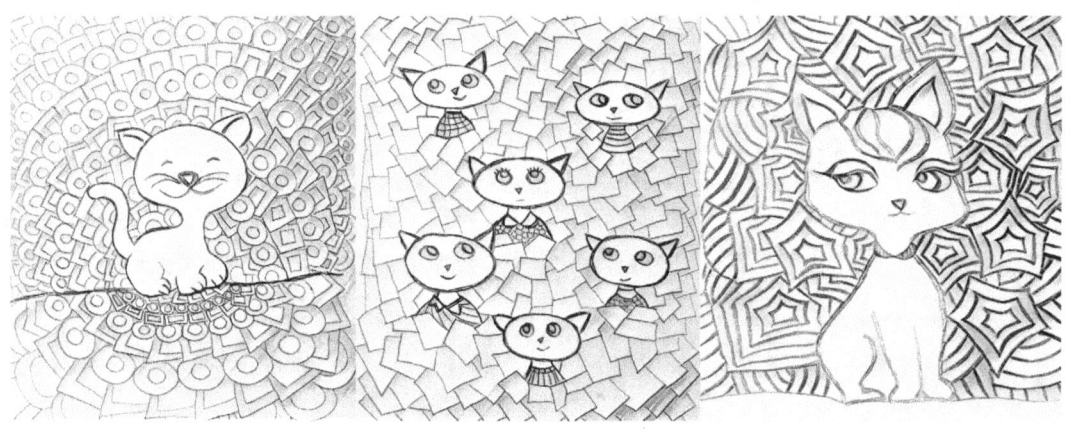

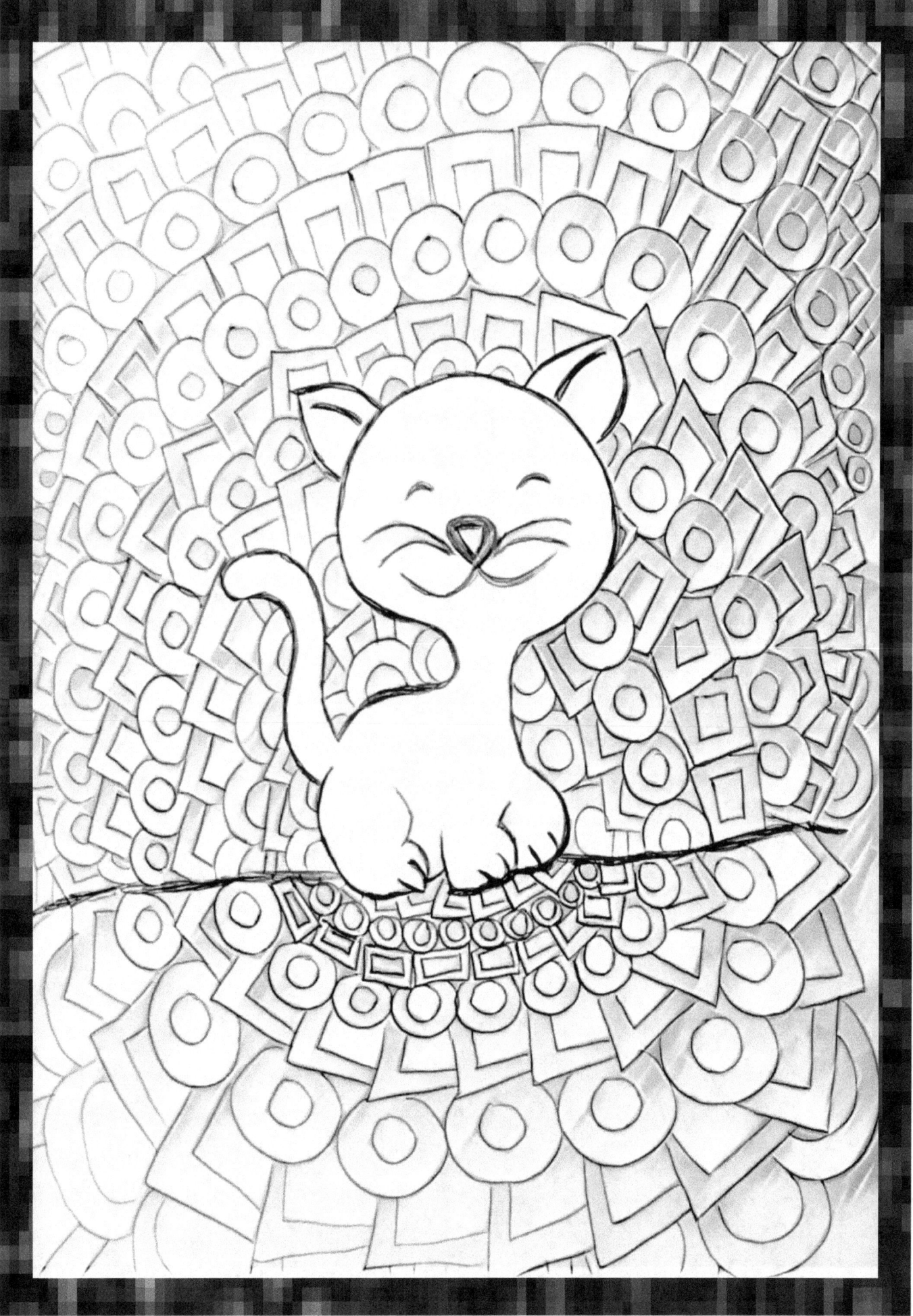

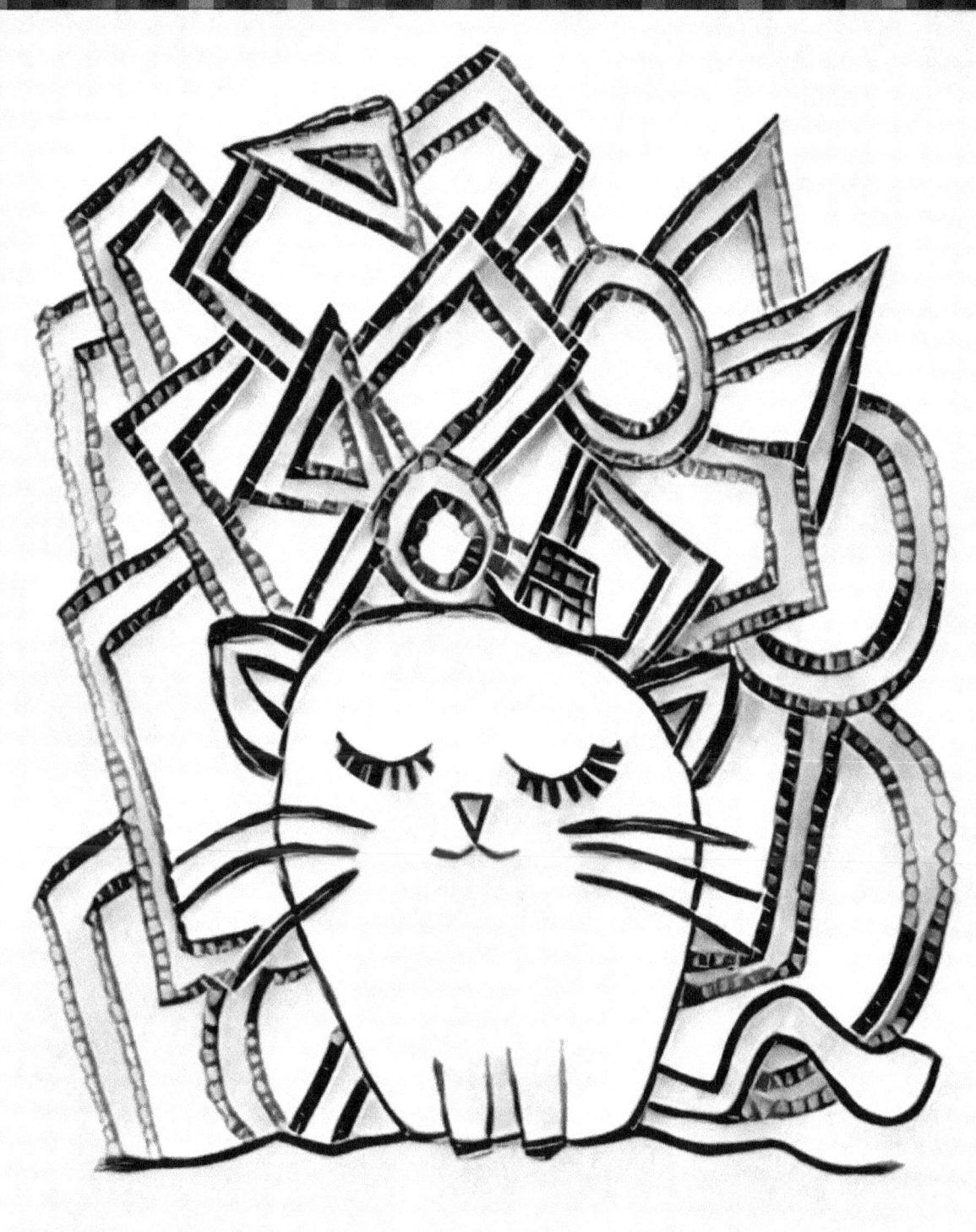

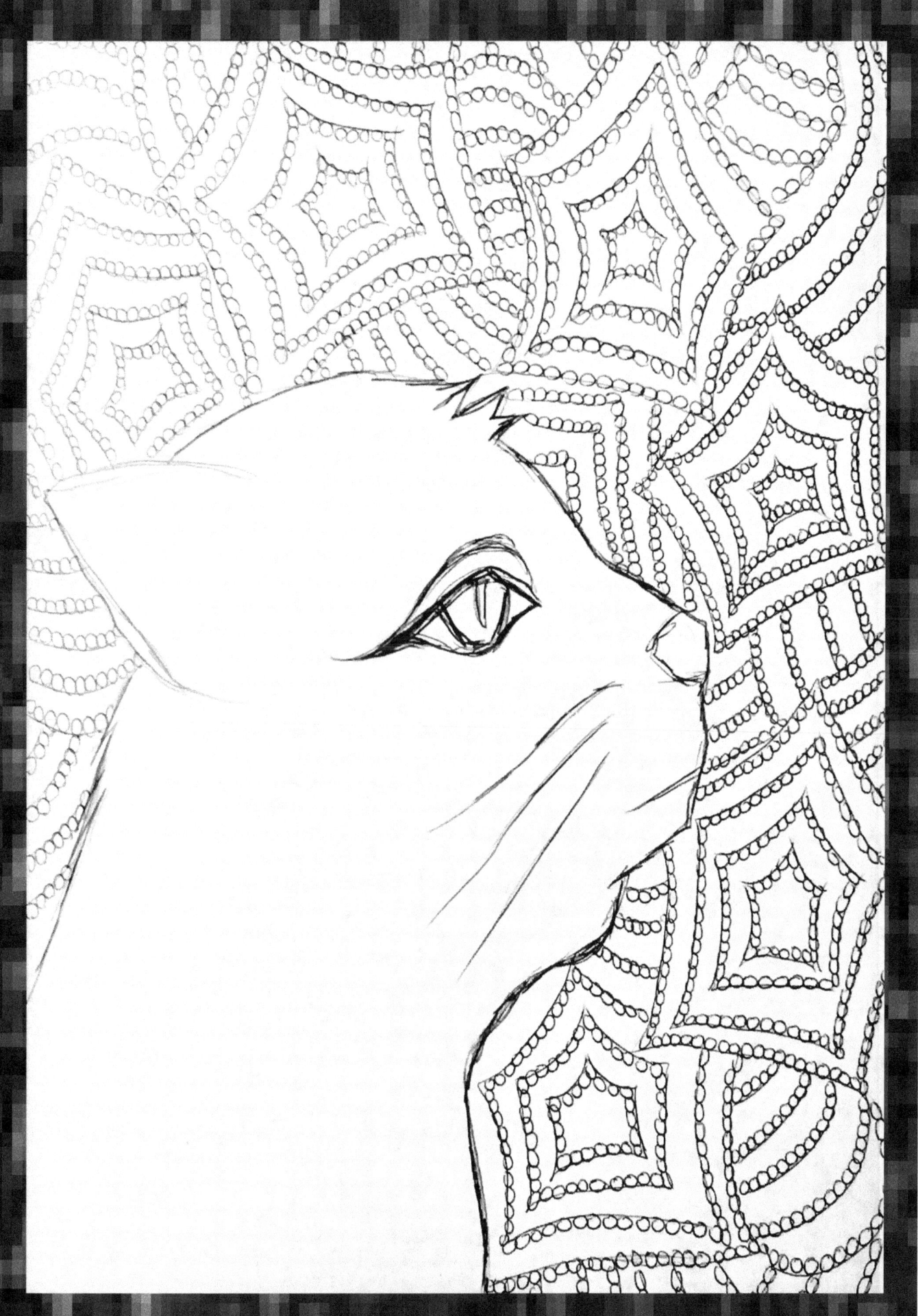

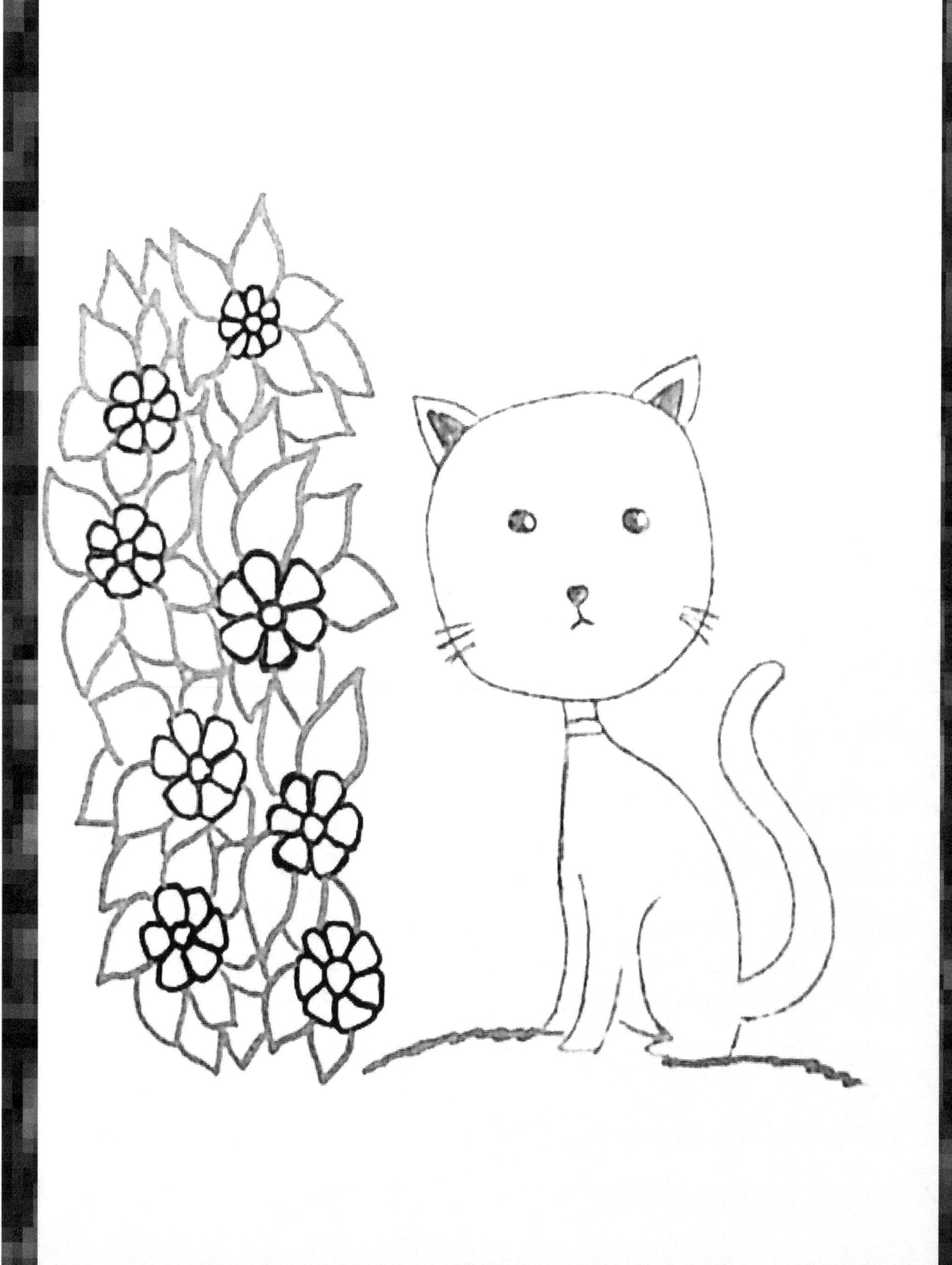

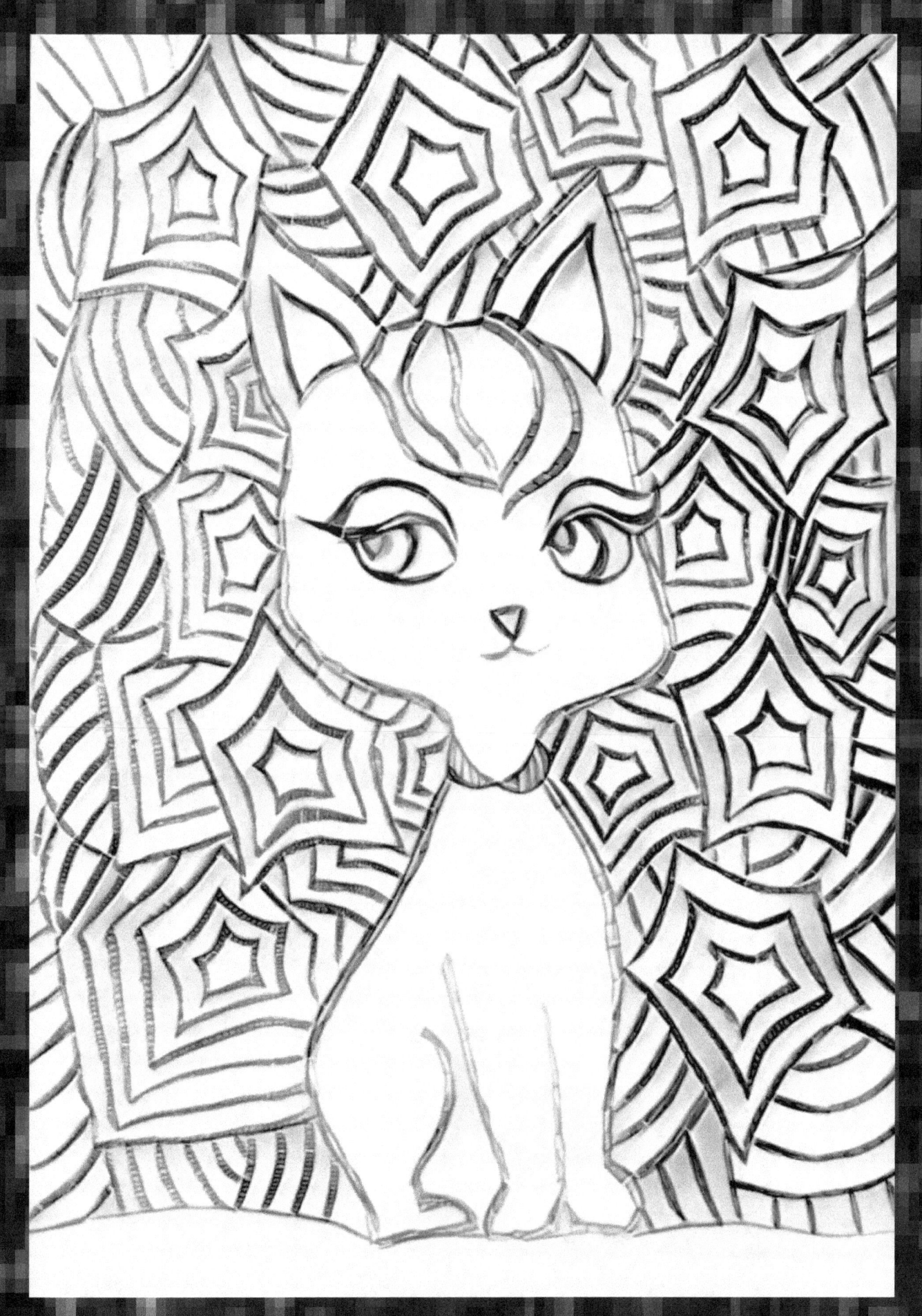

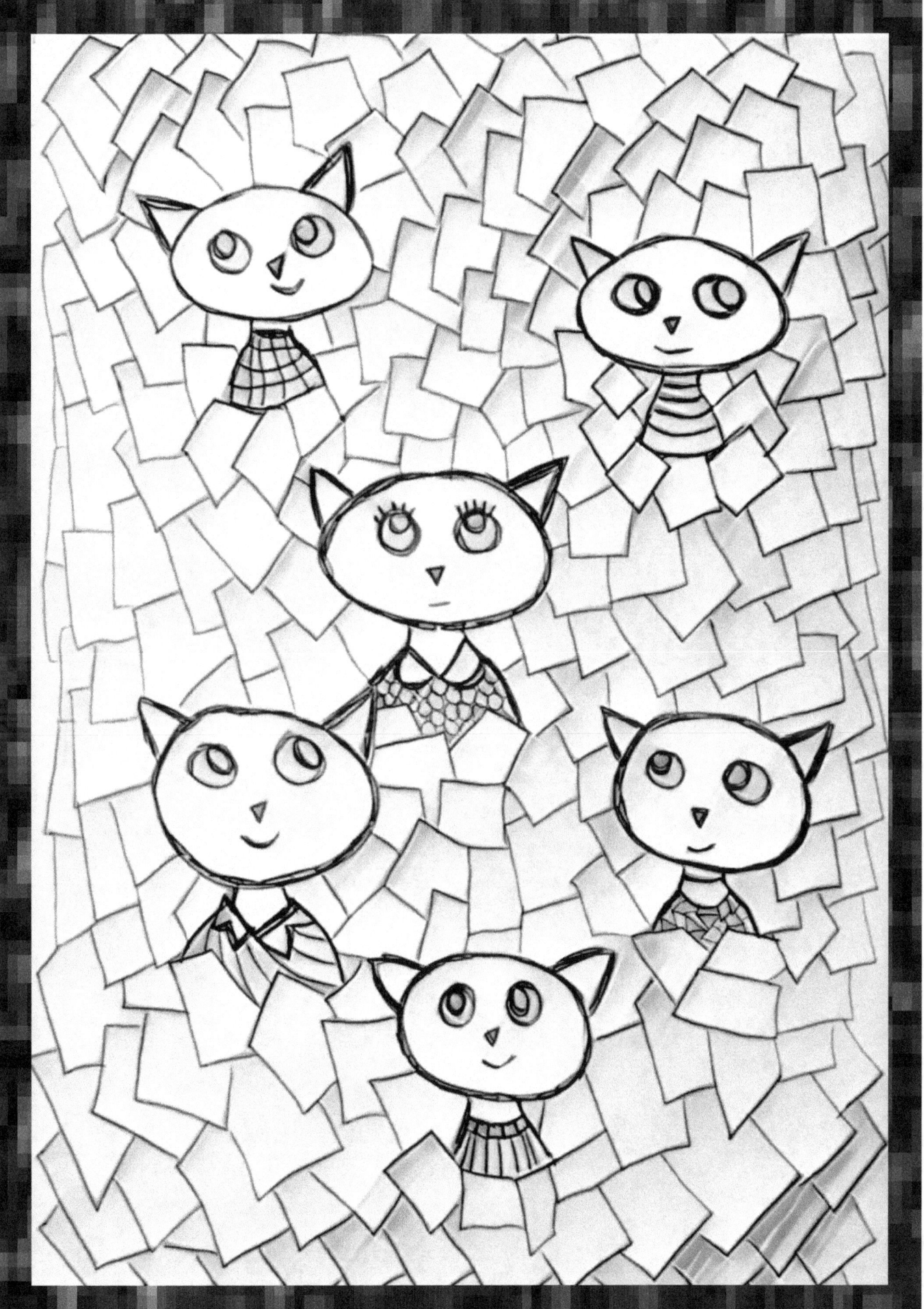

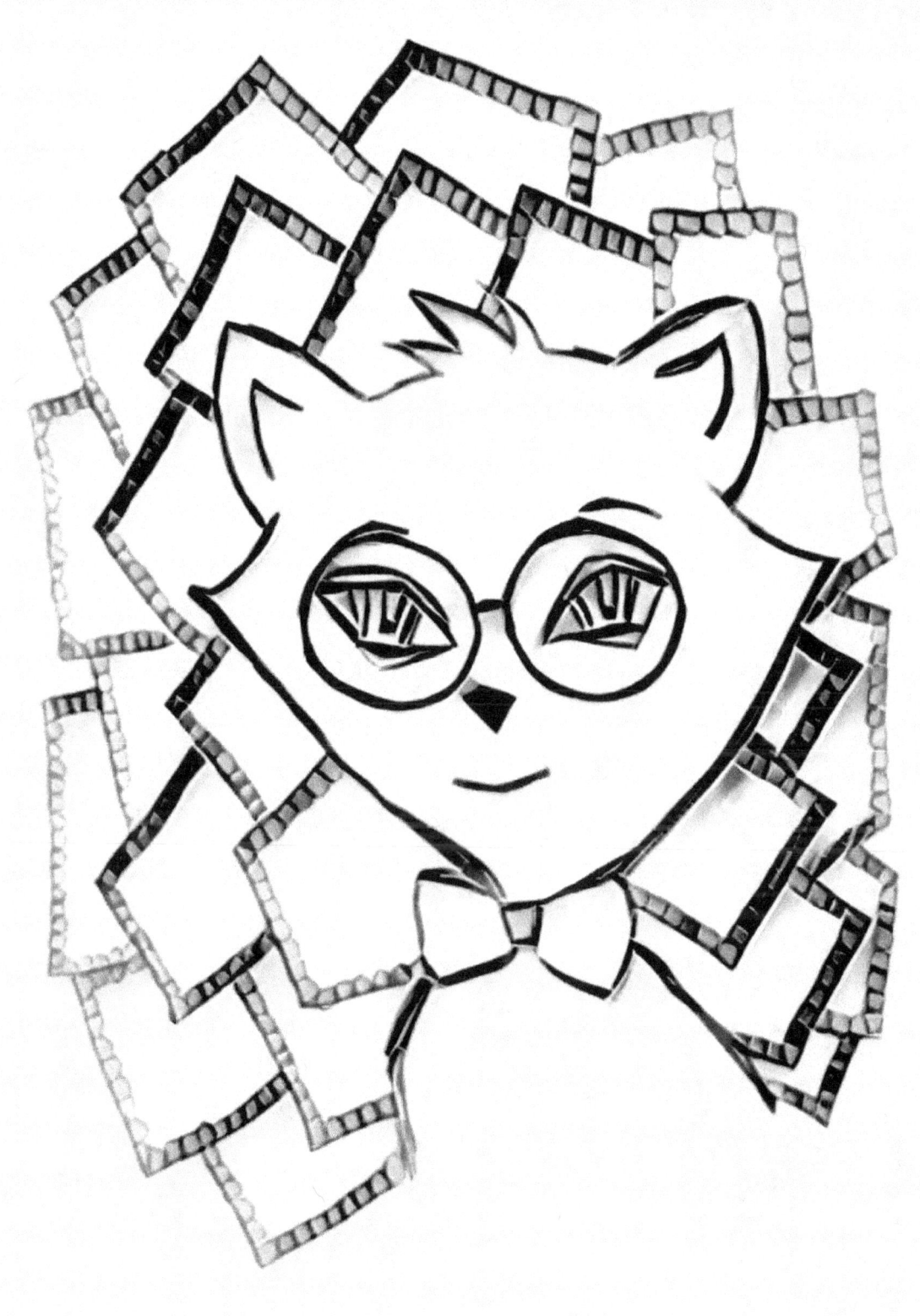

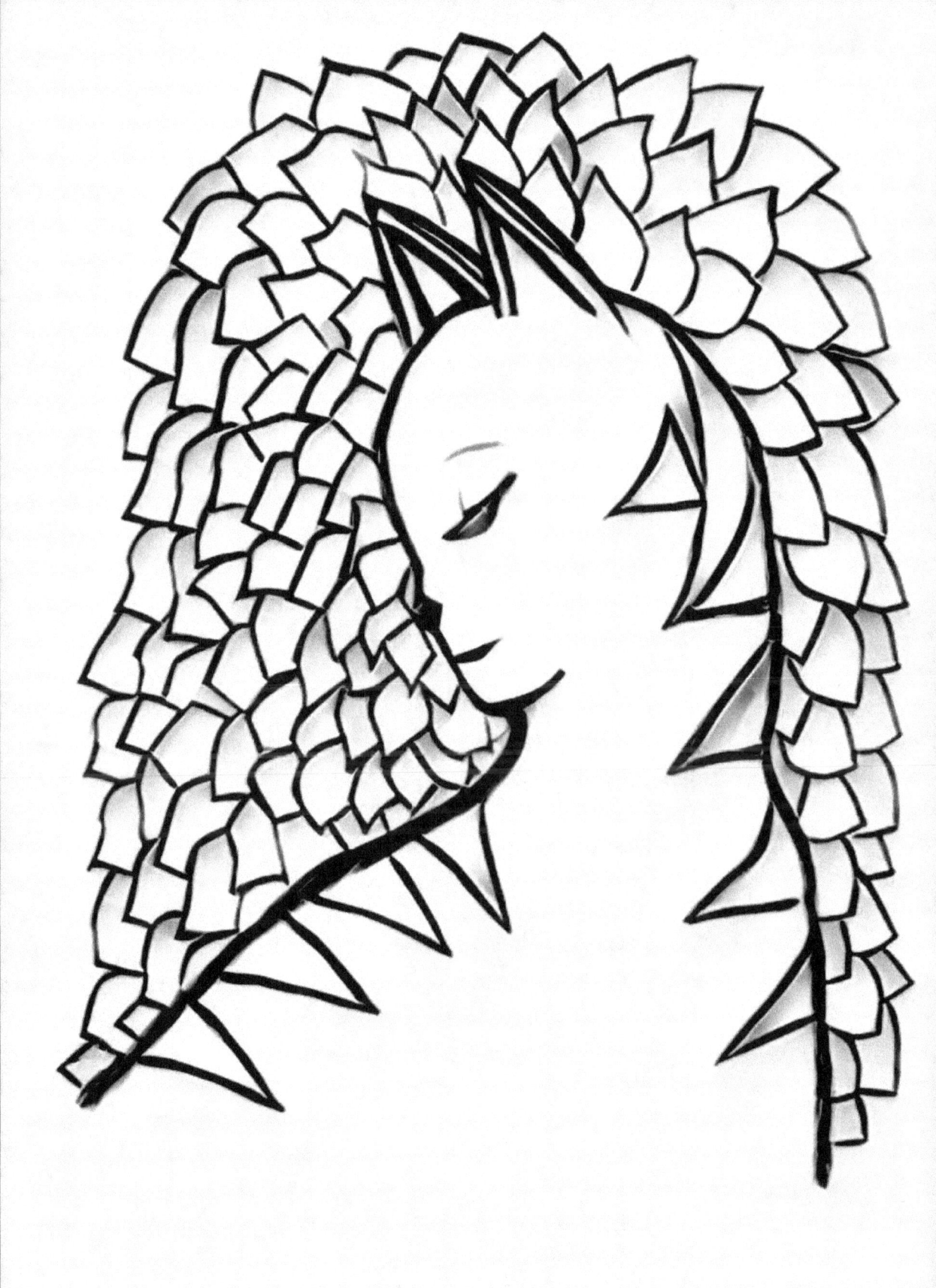

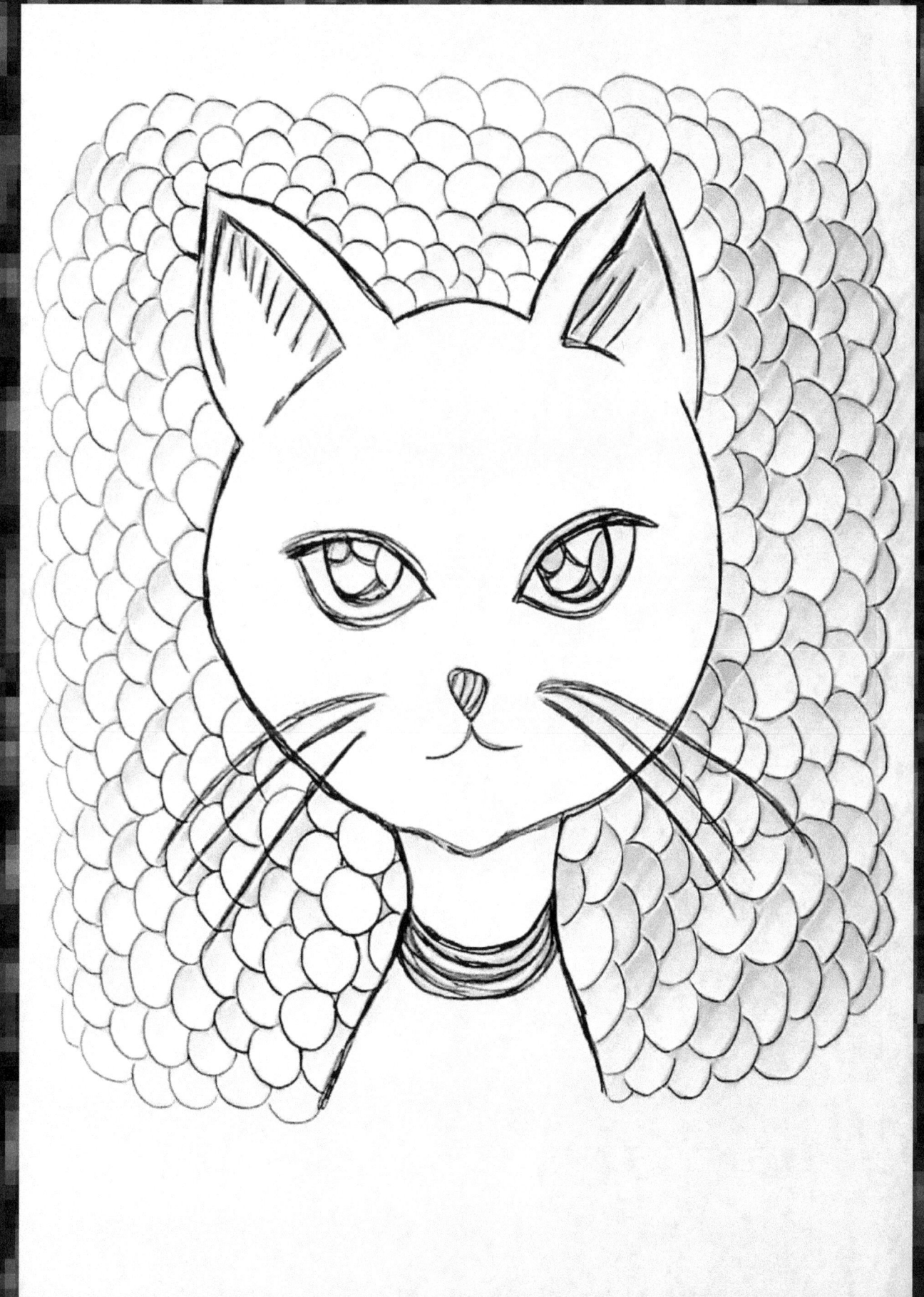

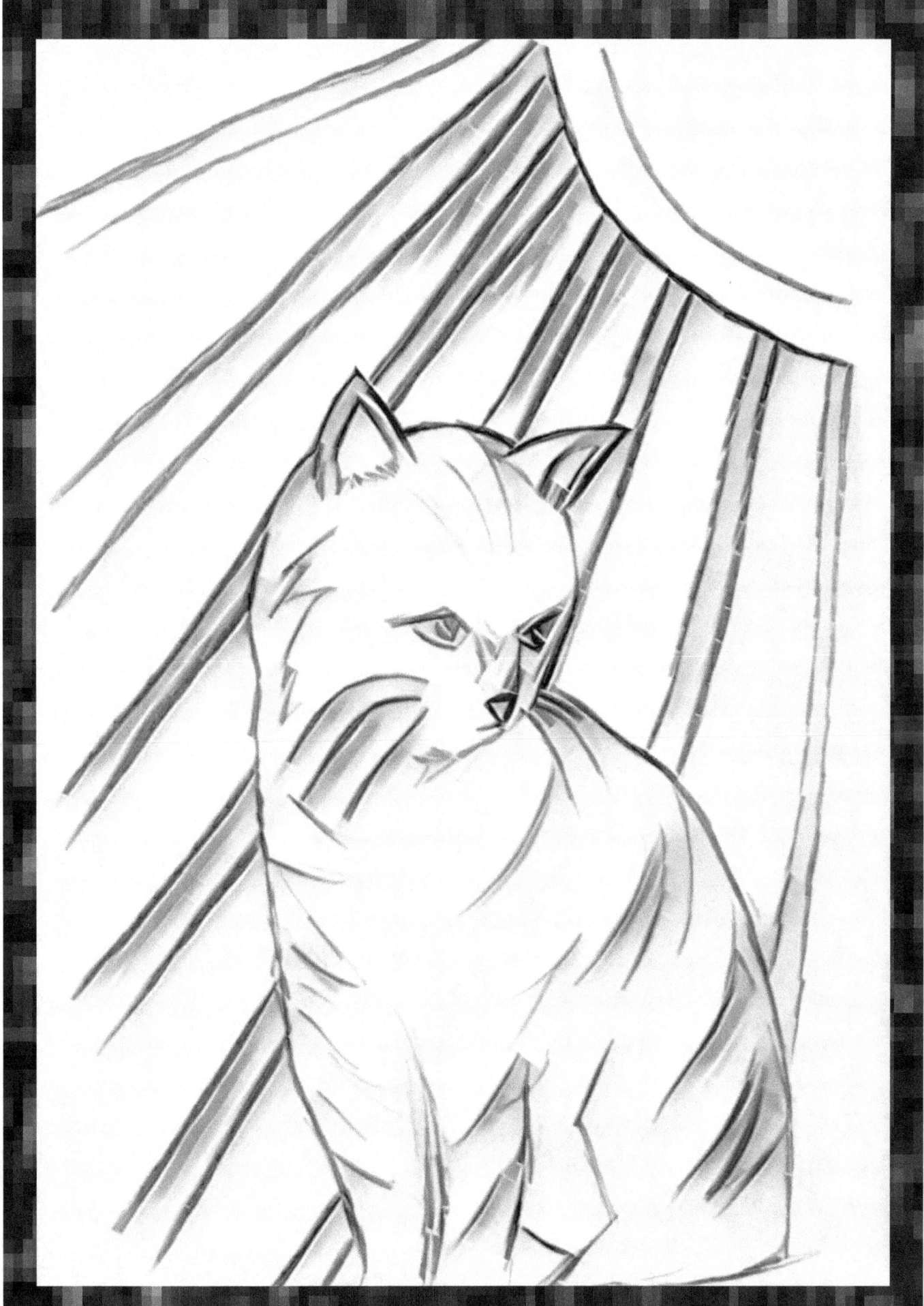

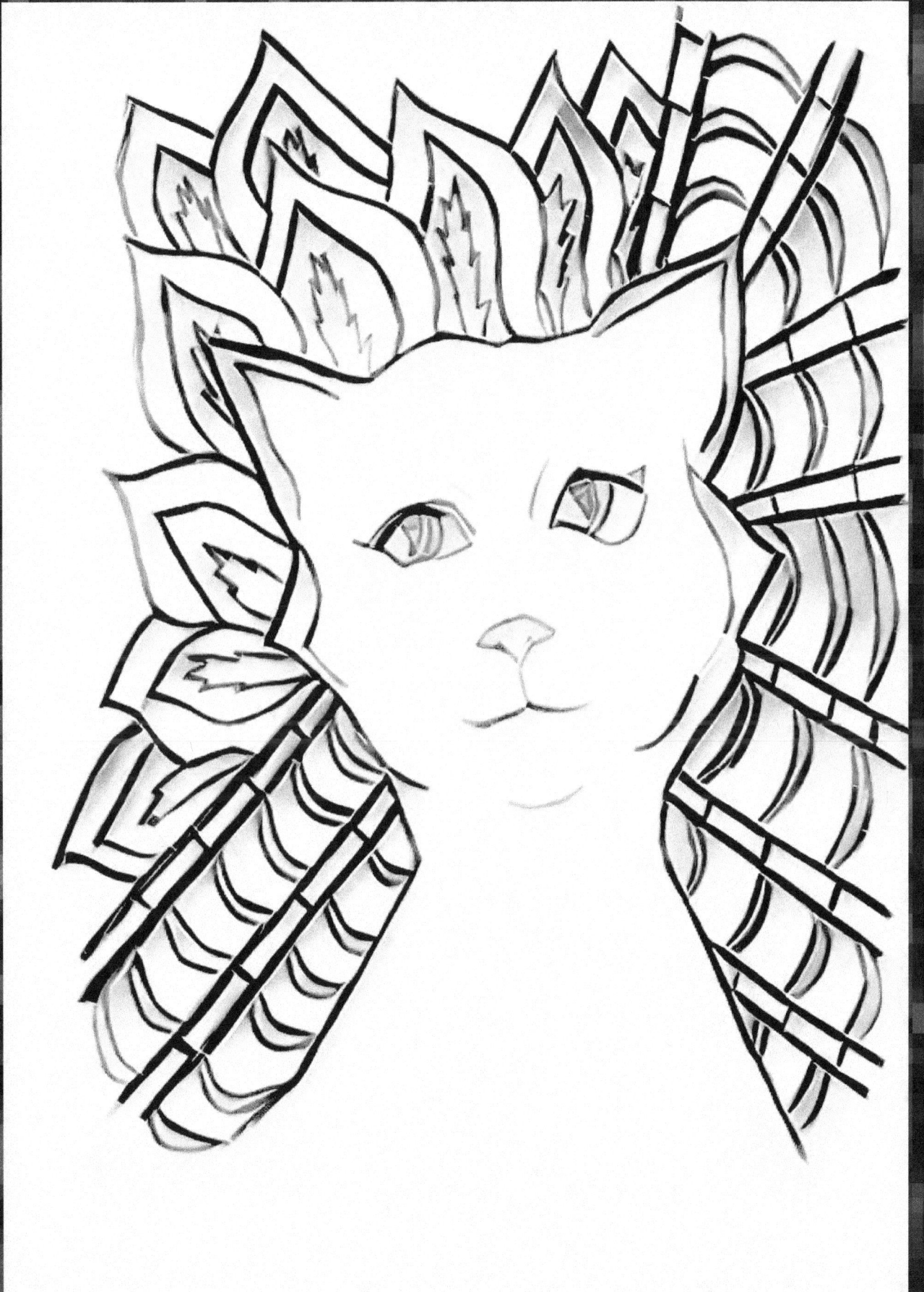

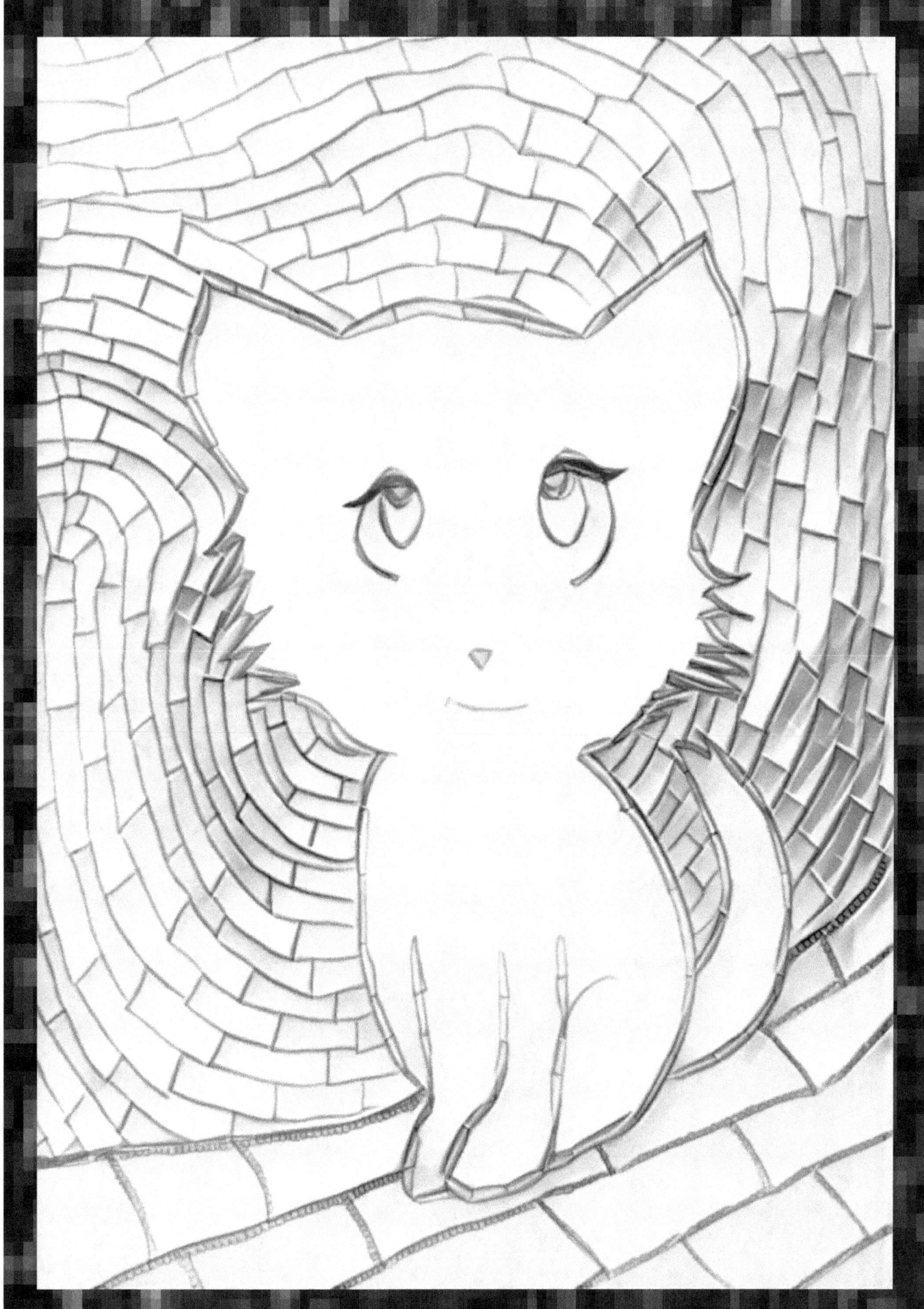

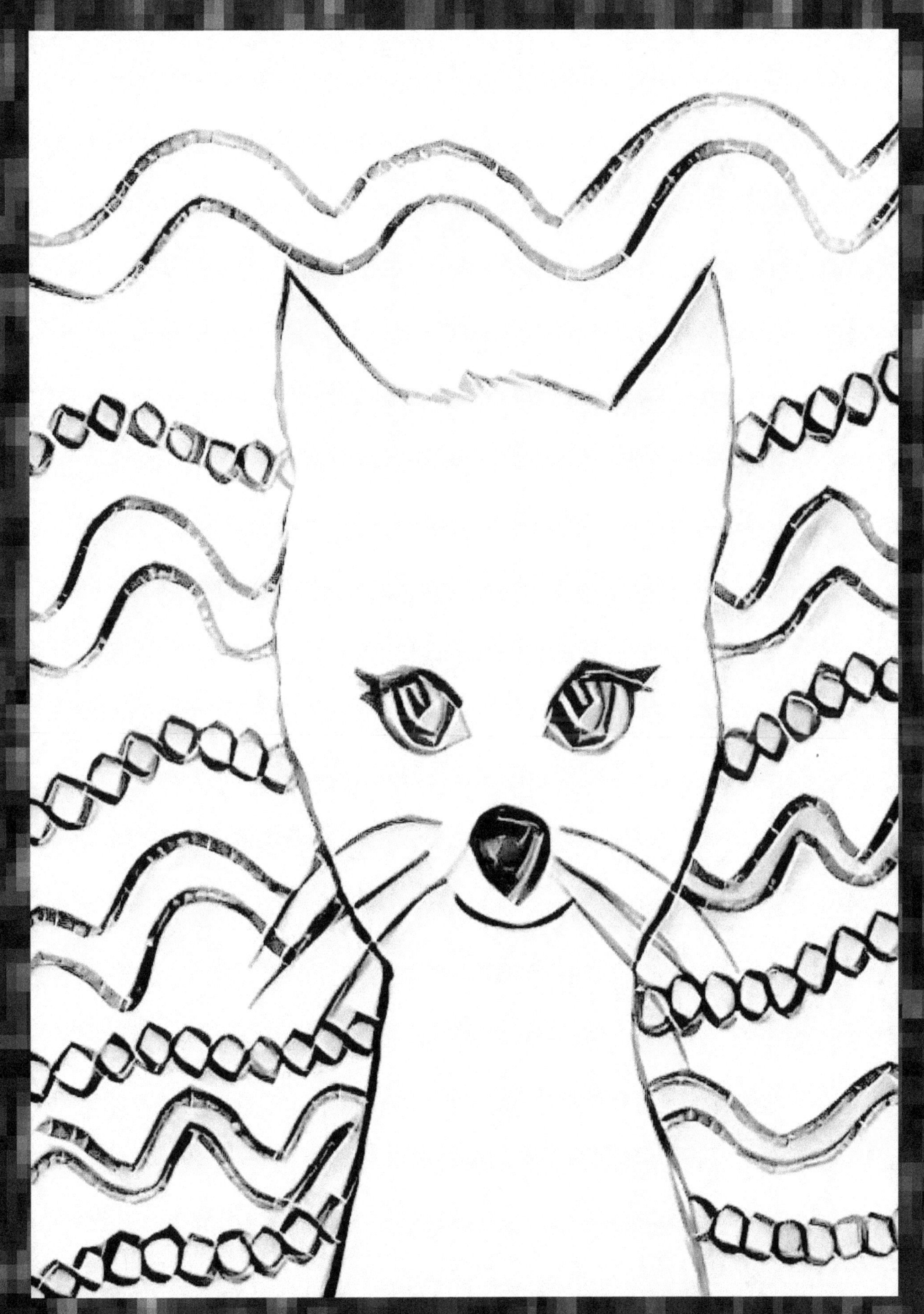

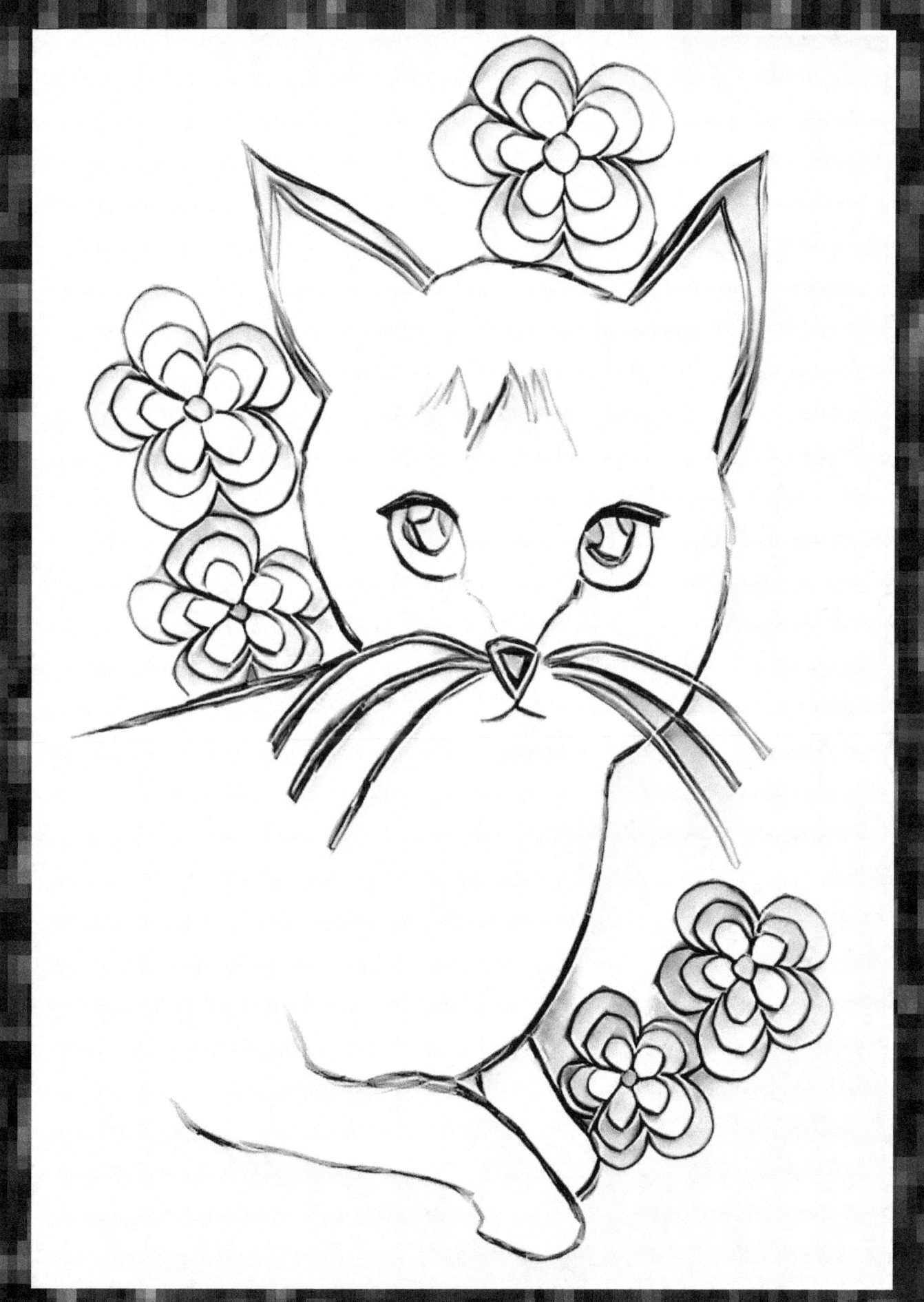

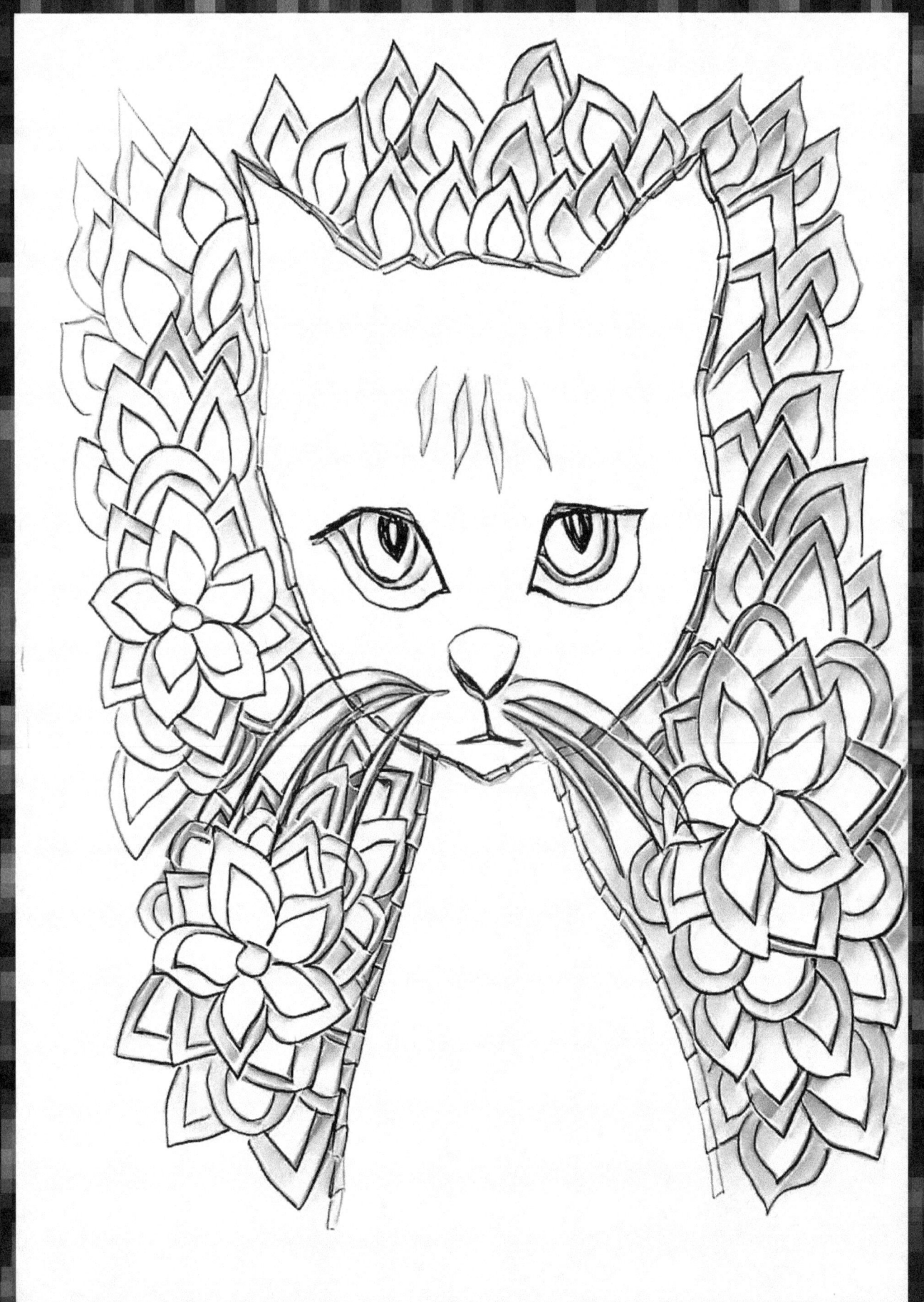

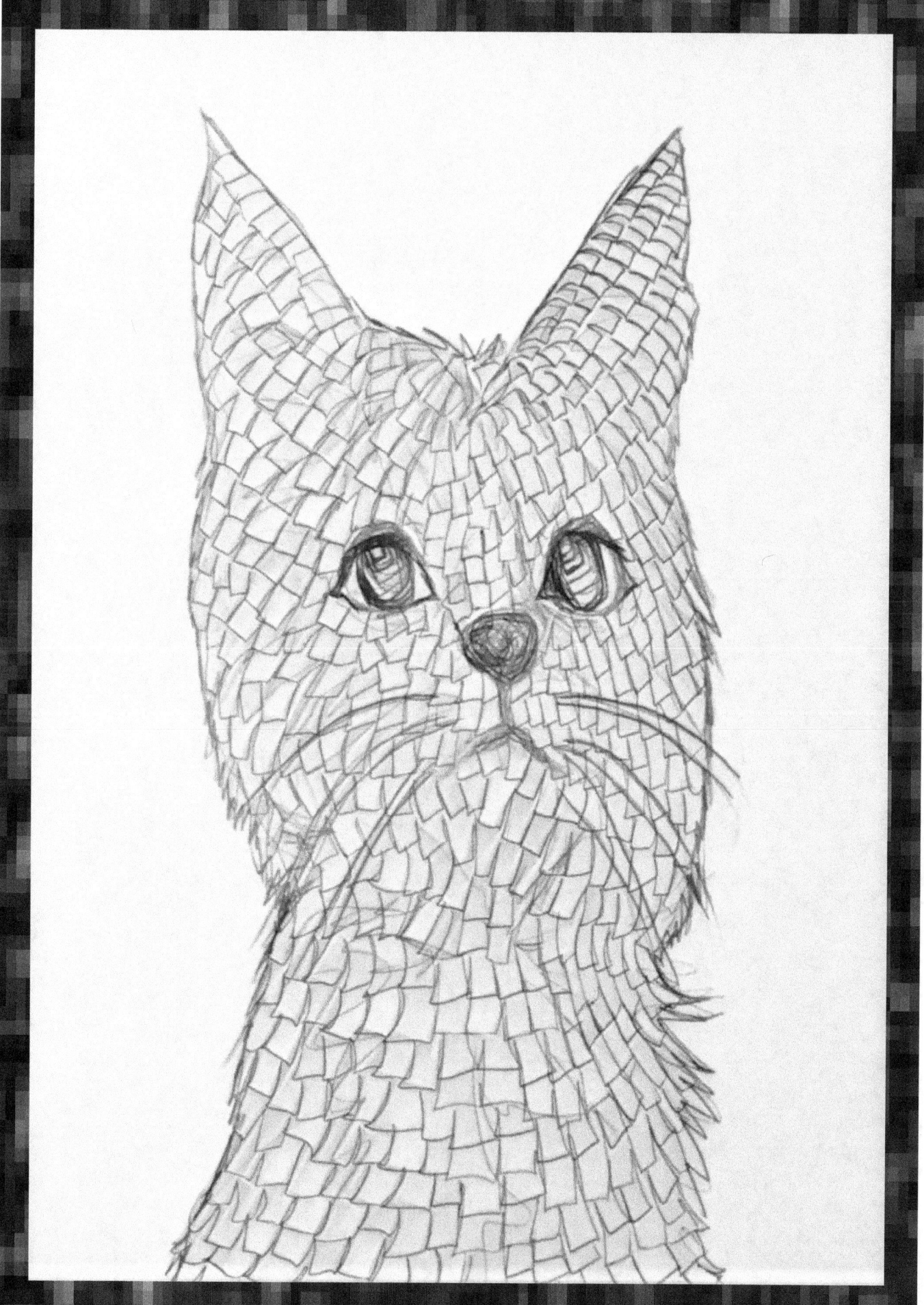

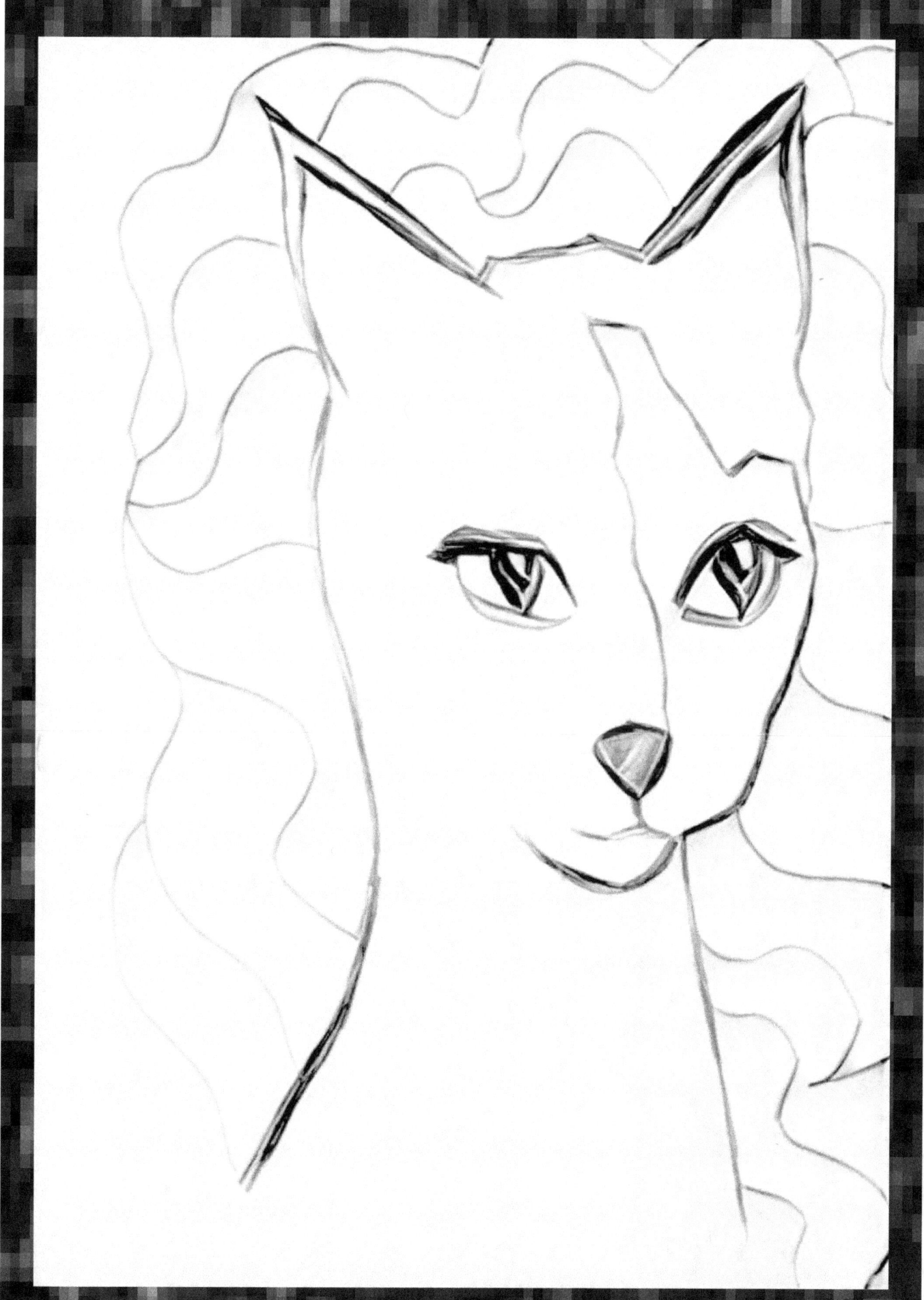

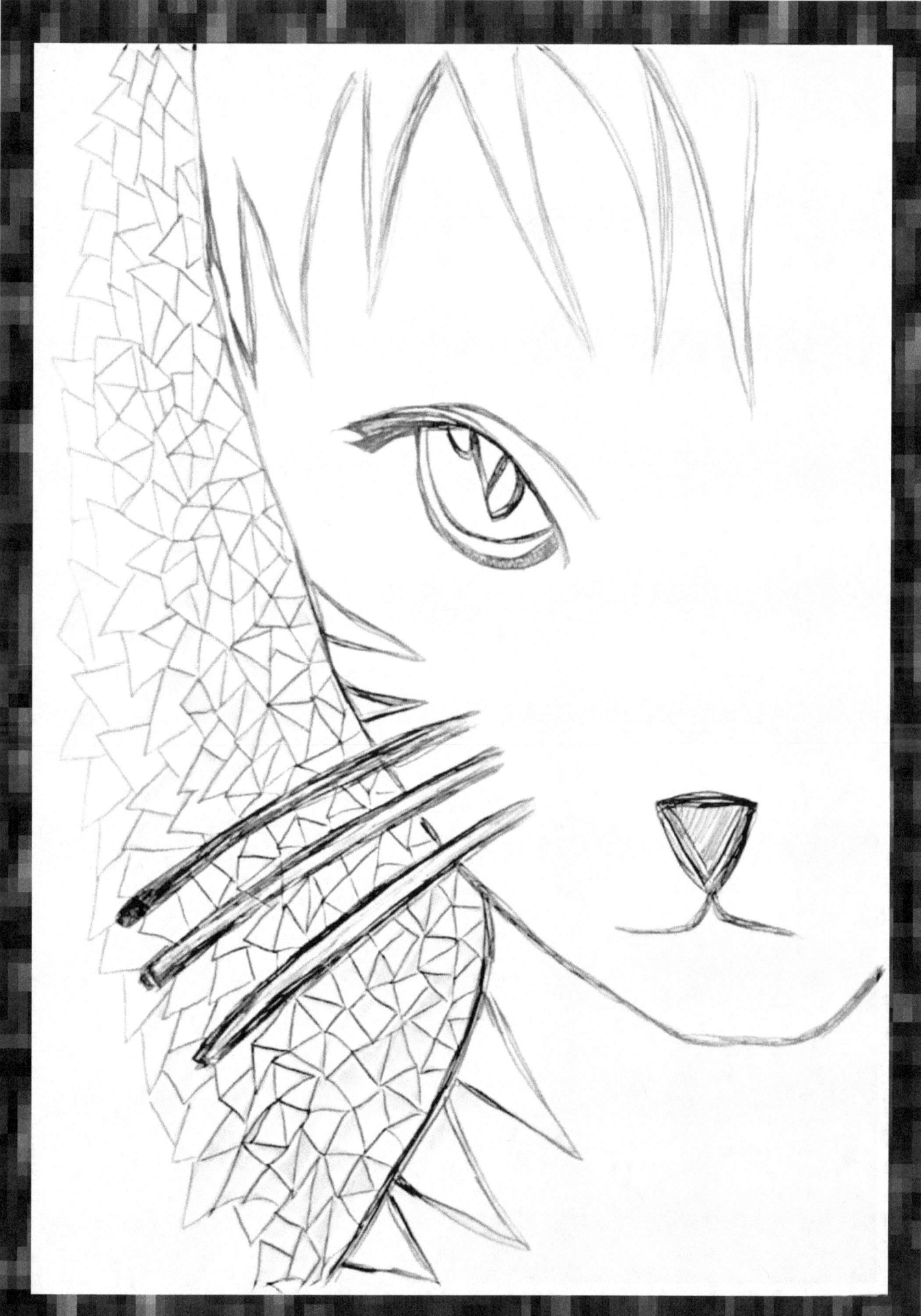

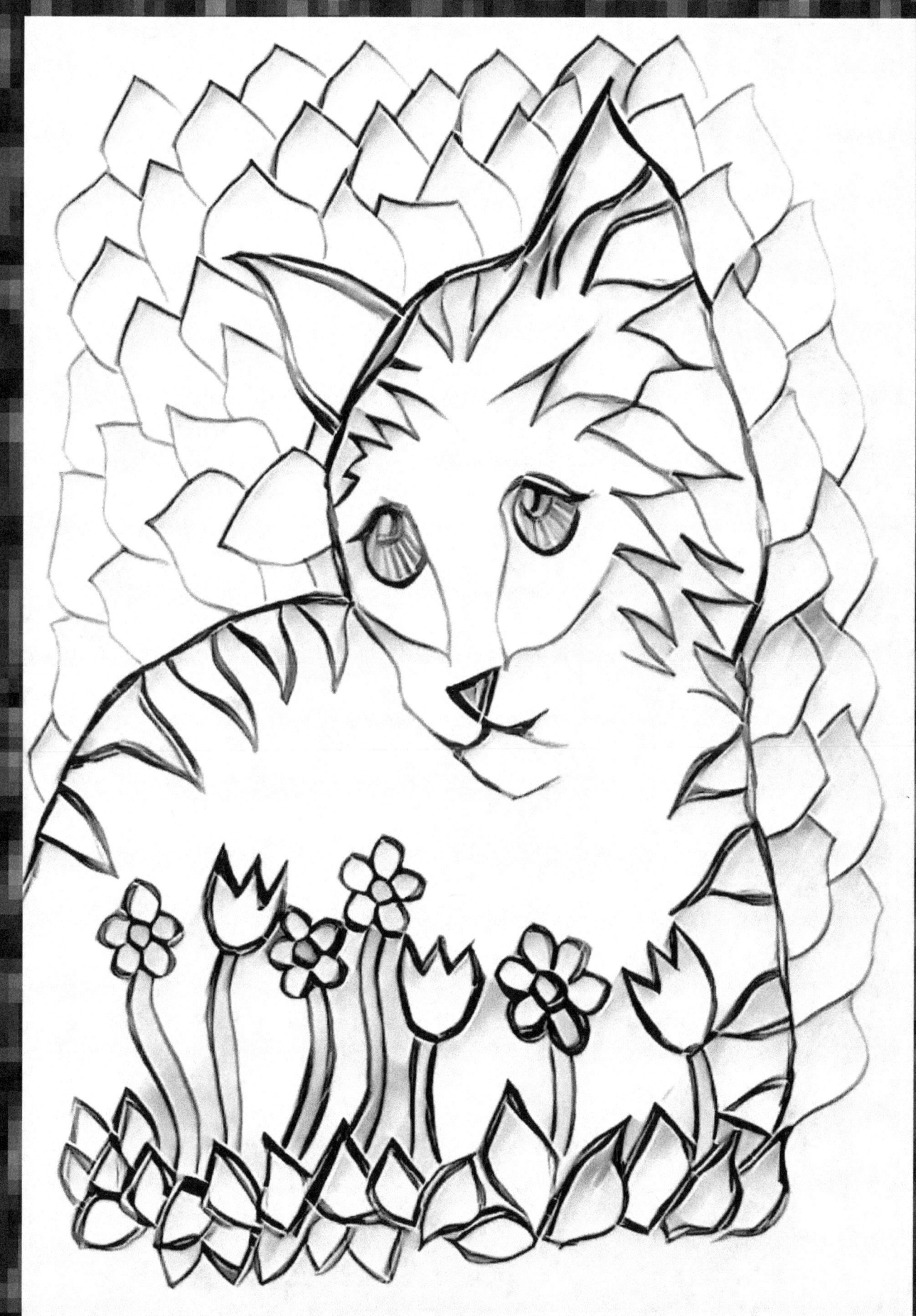

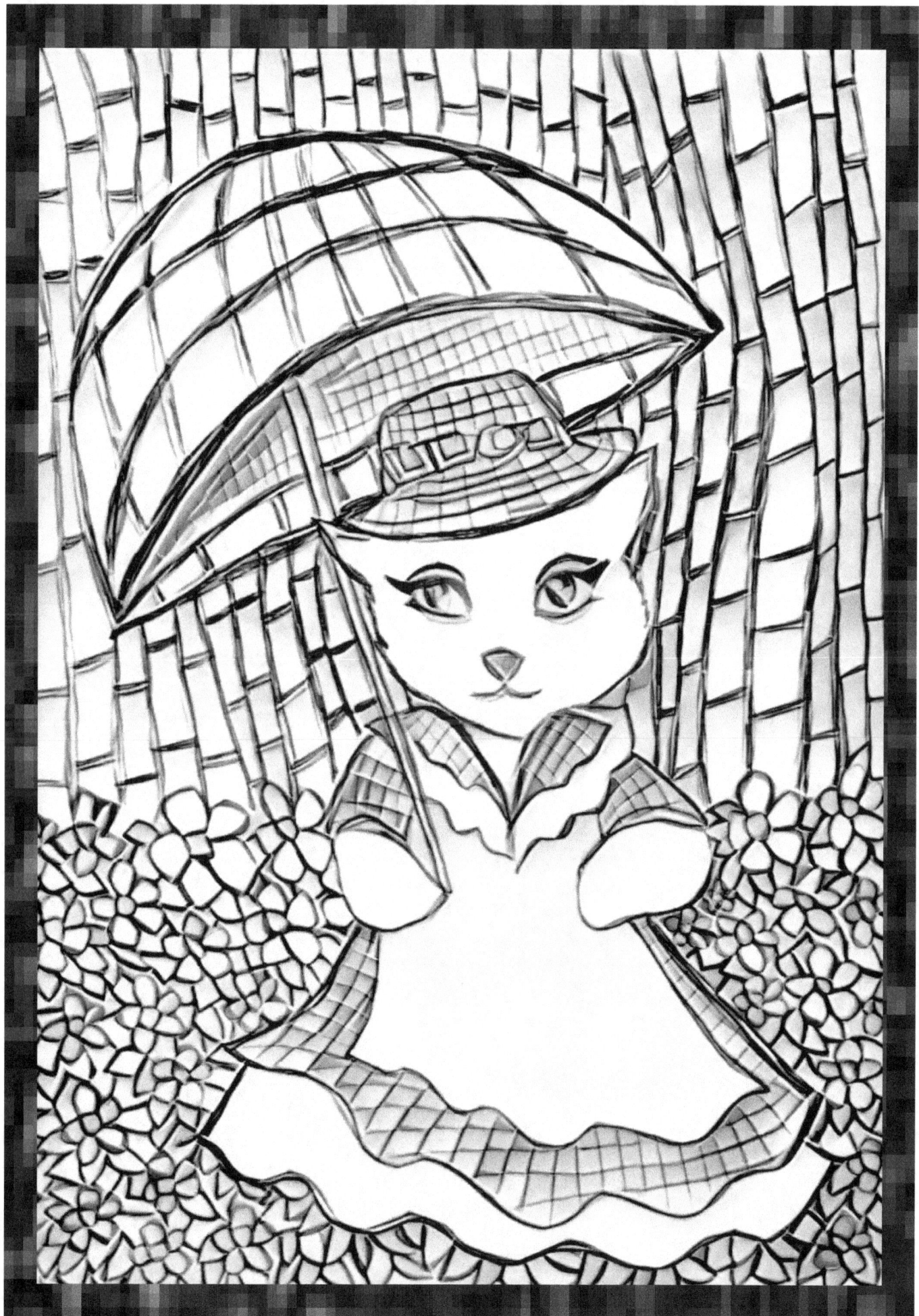

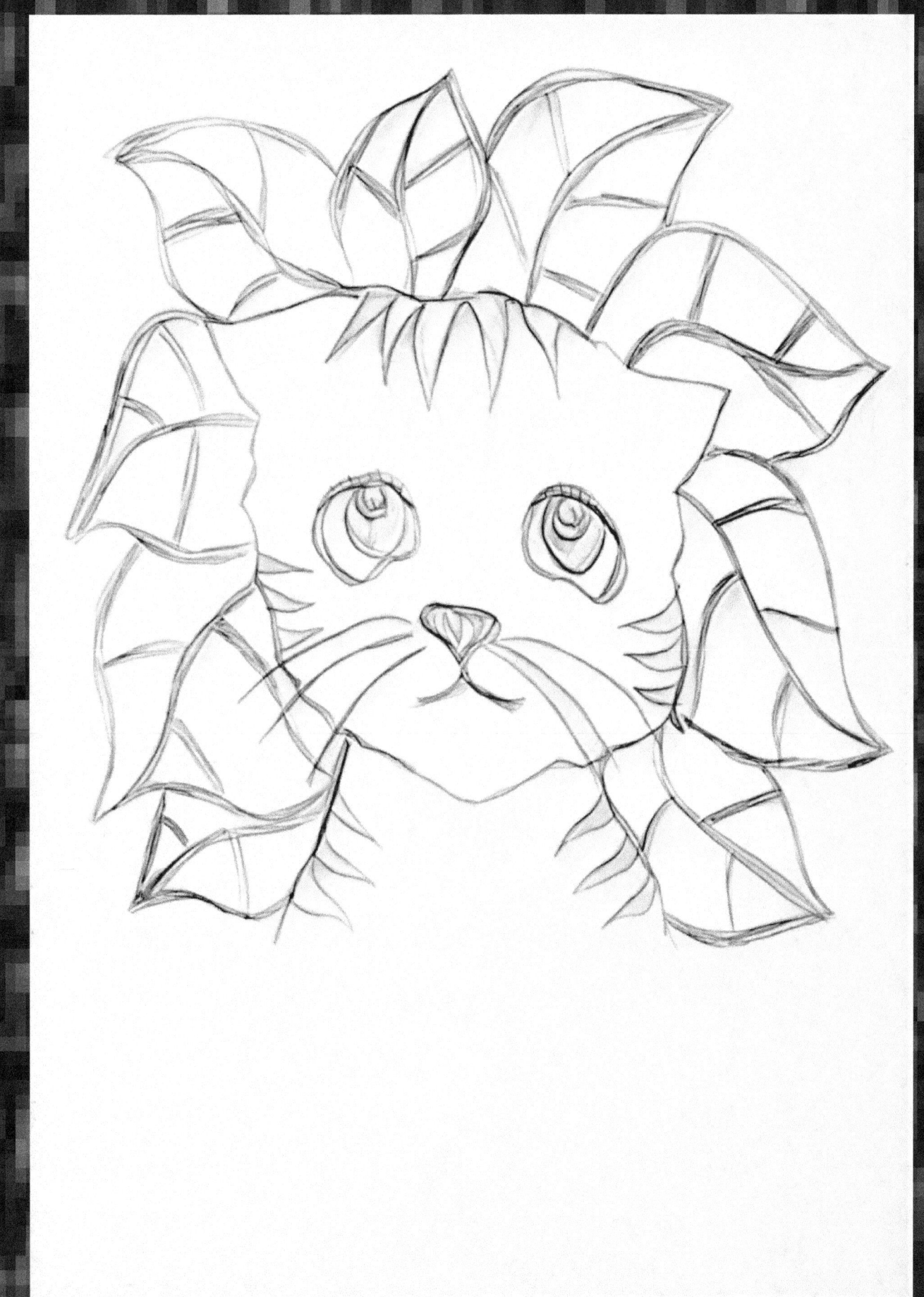

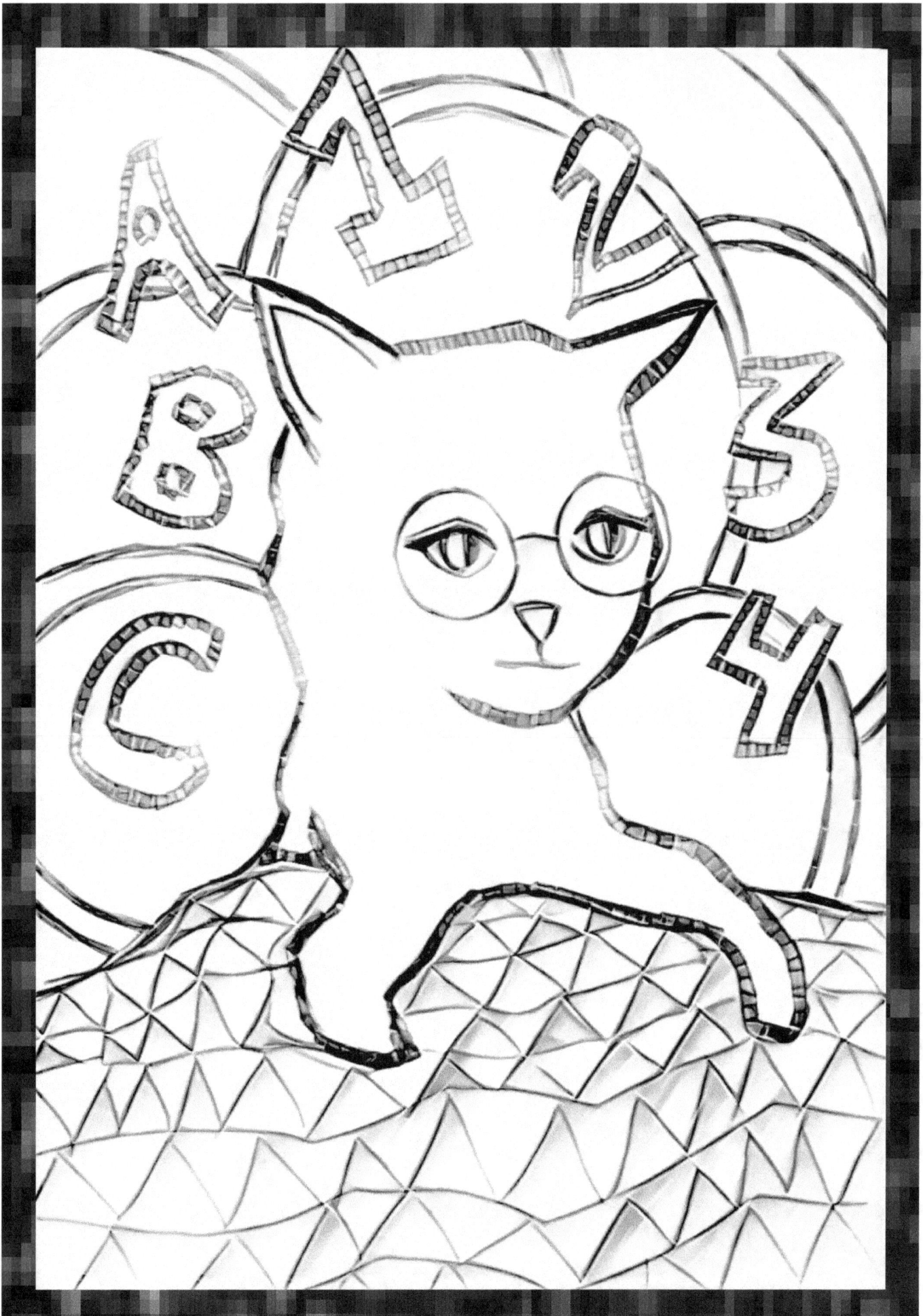

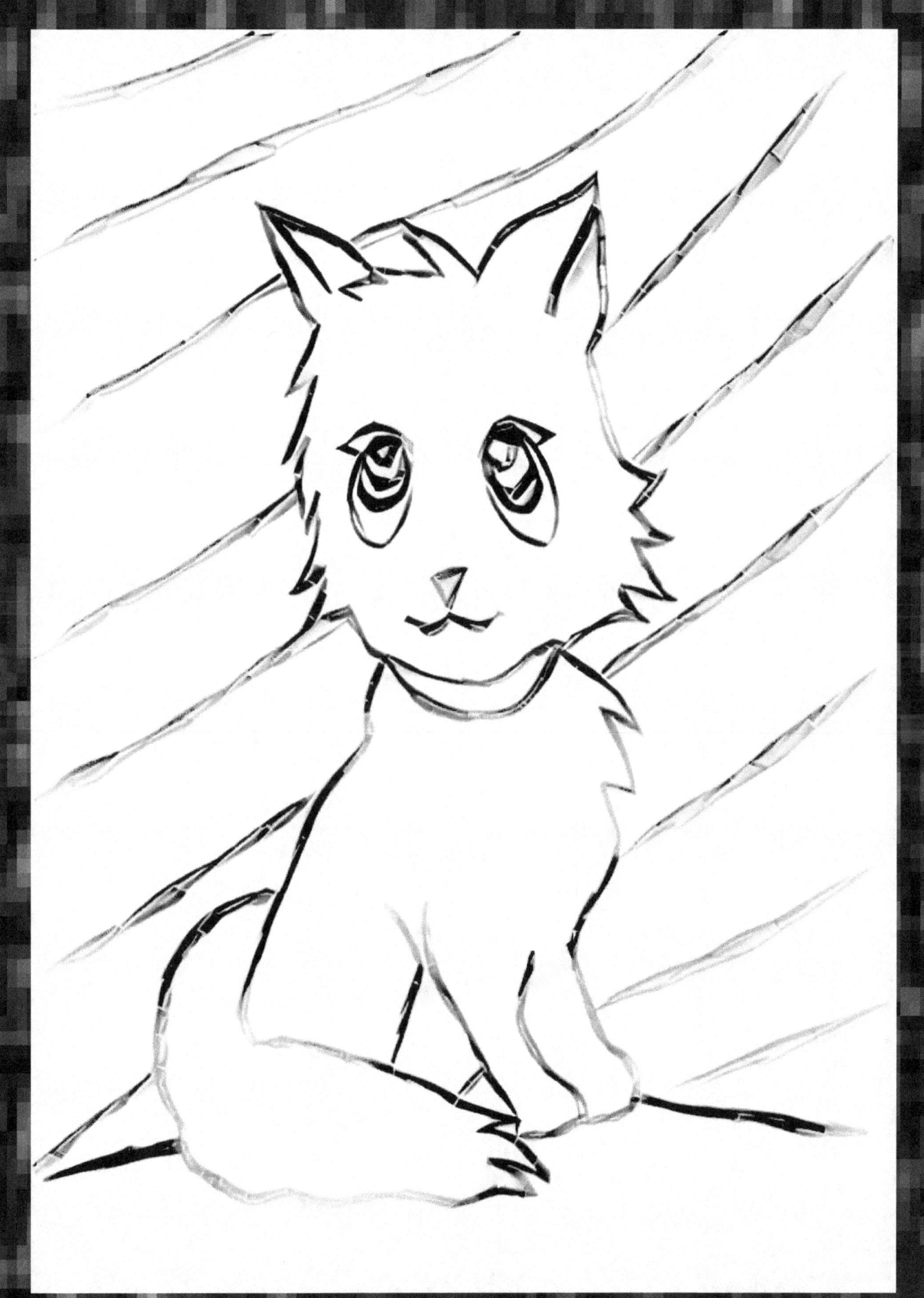

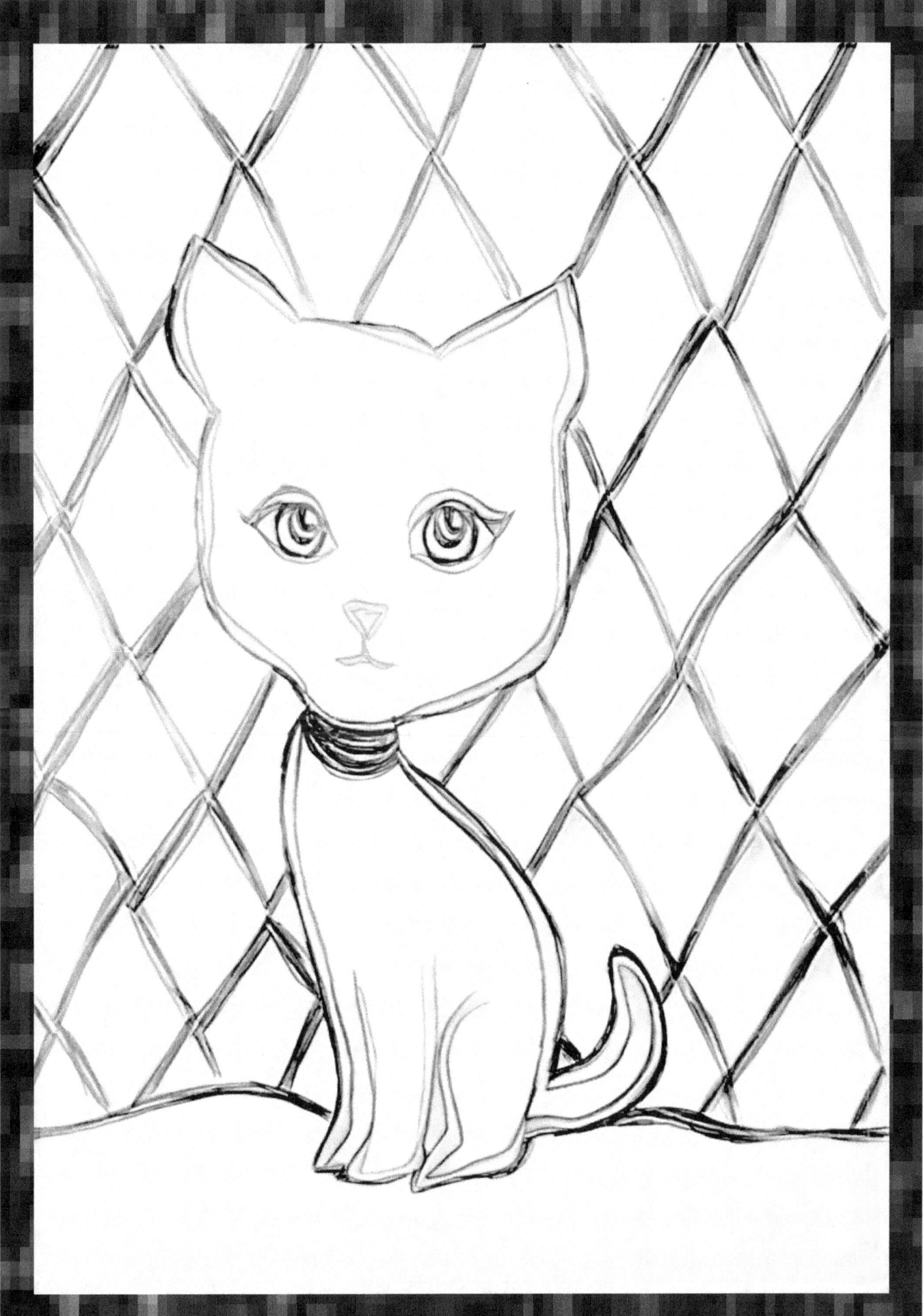

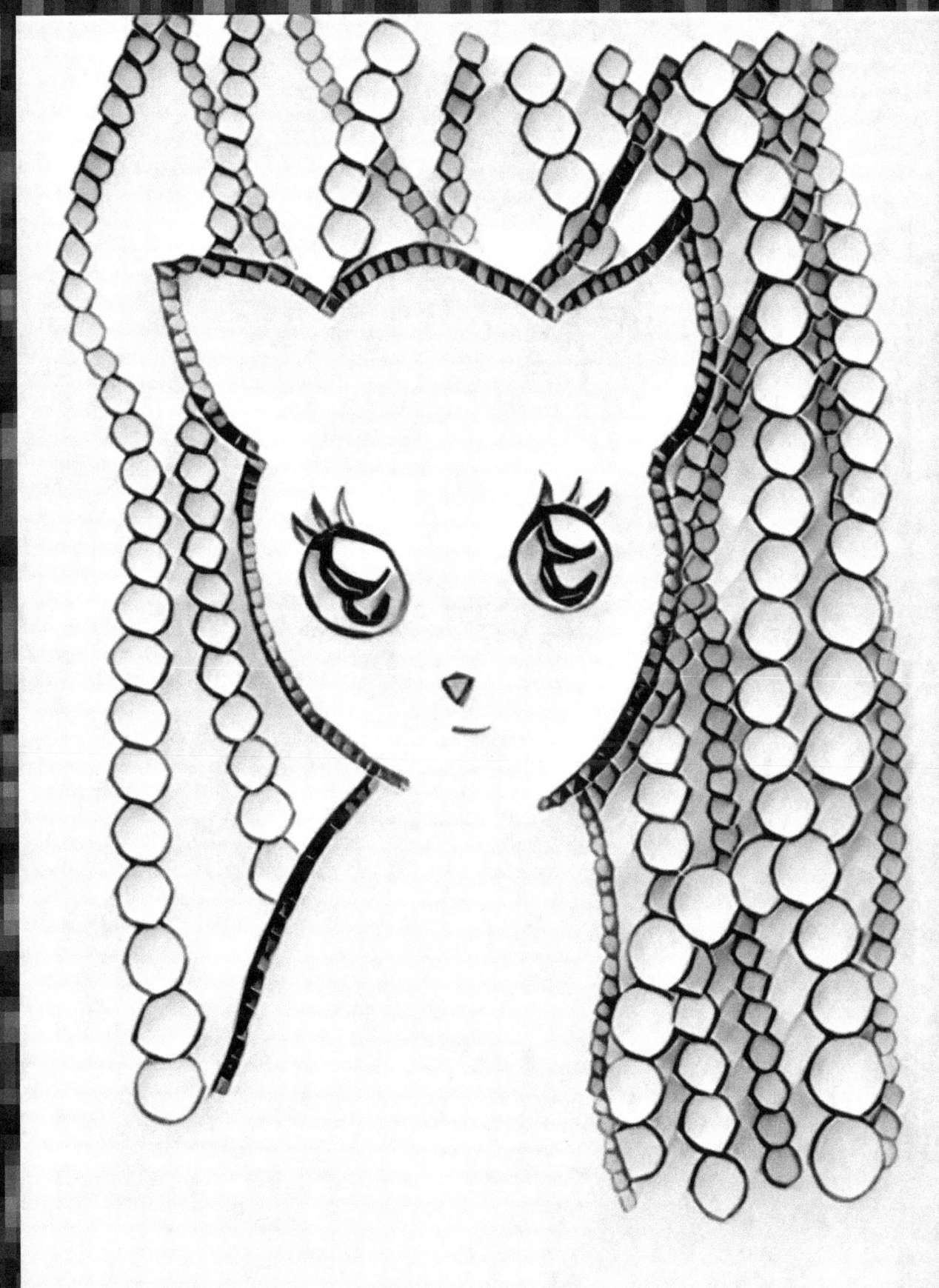

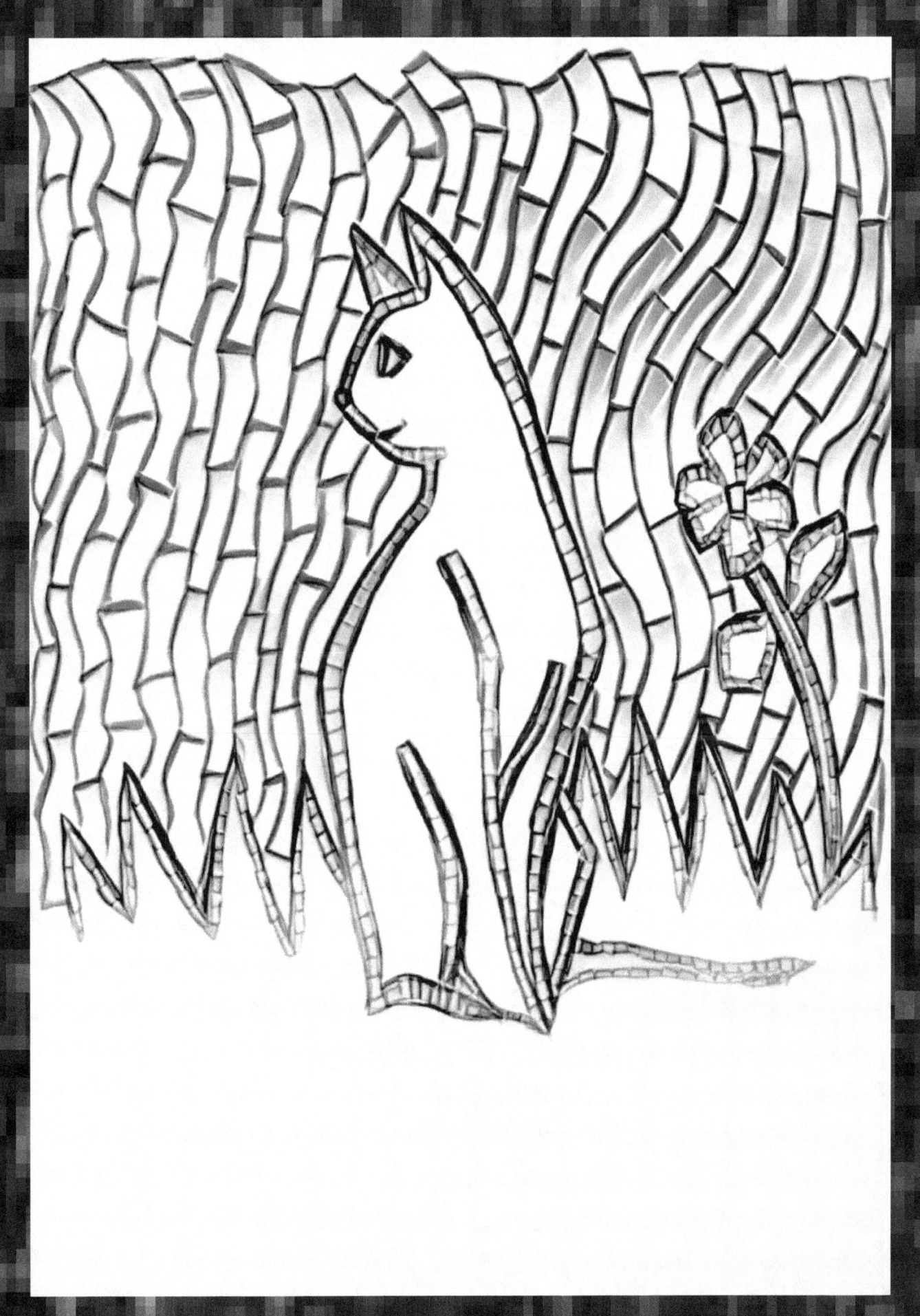

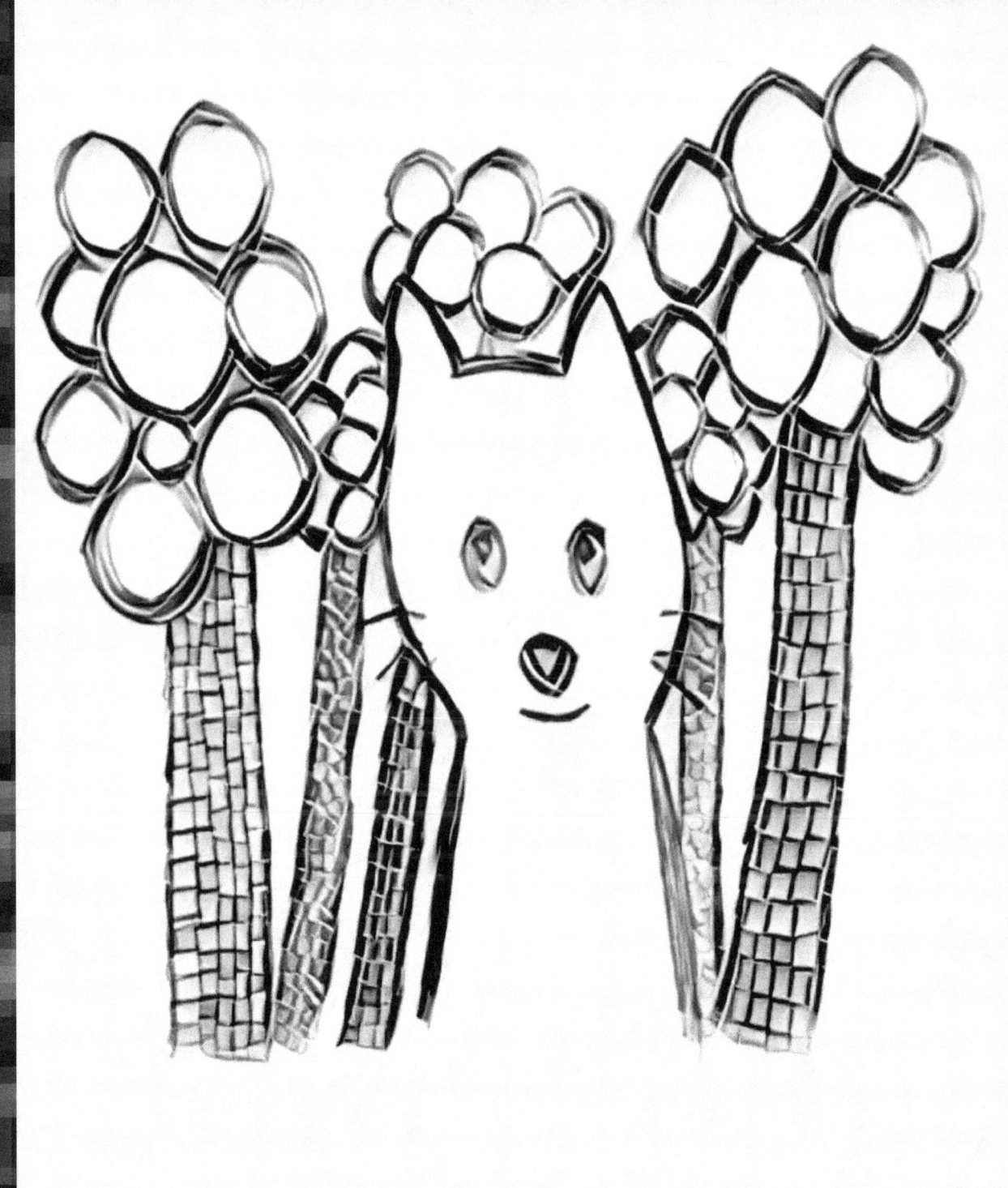

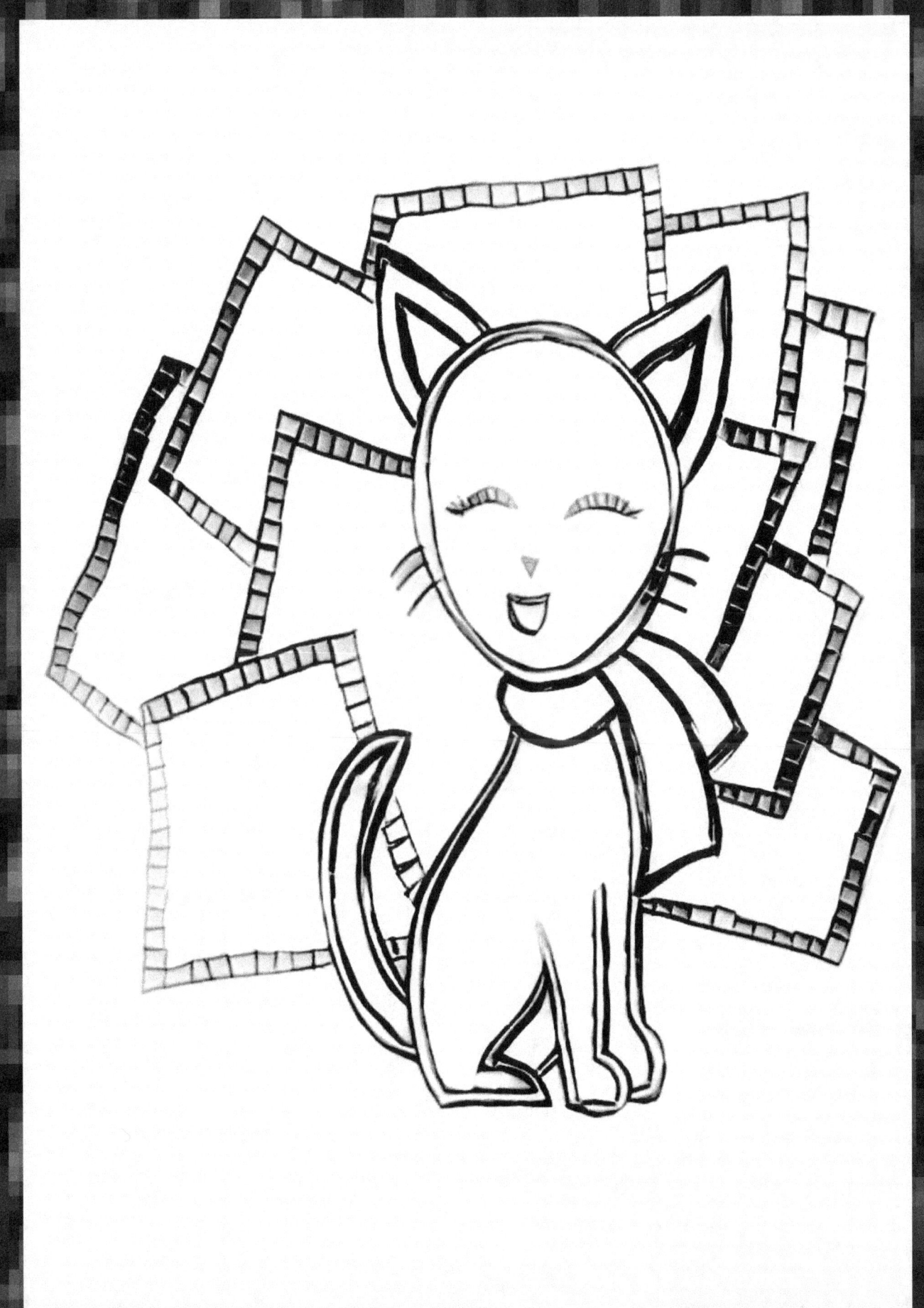

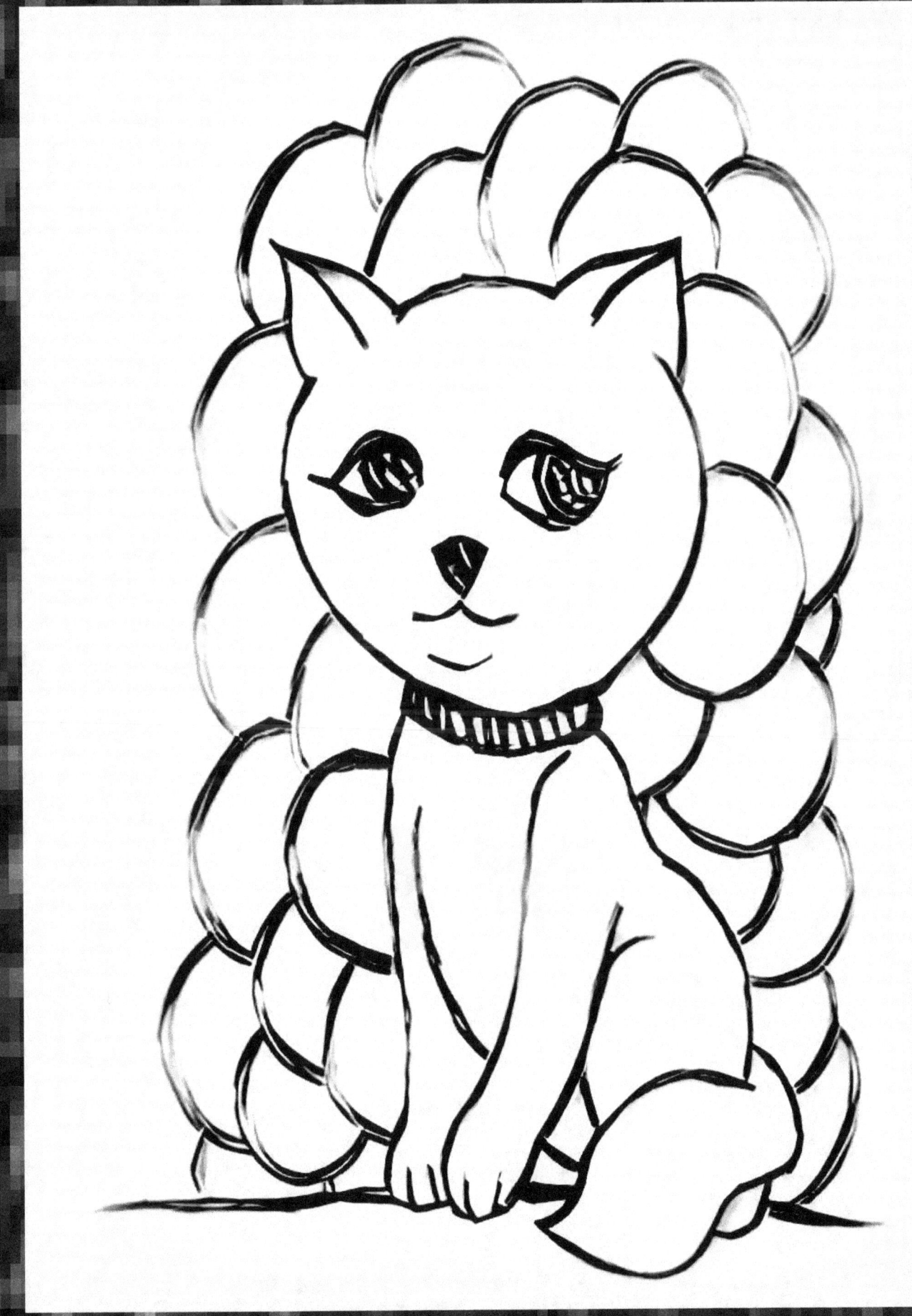

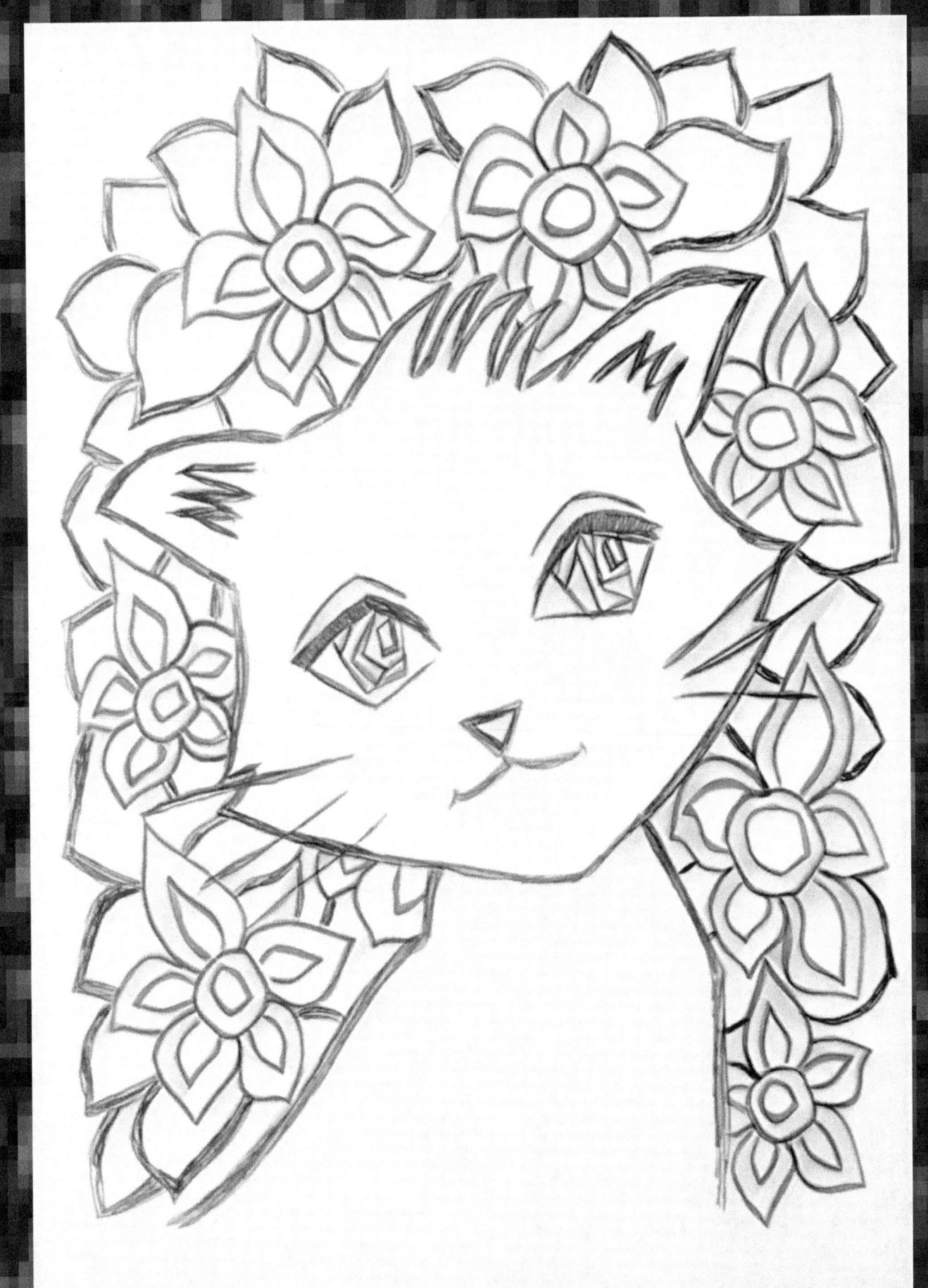

www.ingramcontent.com/pod-product-compliance
Lightning Source LLC
Chambersburg PA
CBHW062231220526
45471CB00009B/3428